DELIBERATE COACHING

UNLOCK YOUR BEST SELF, ONE GOAL AT A TIME

JAVIER ROSALES
JOSE E. GONZATTI

DELIBERATE COACHING

First Edition 2024

ISBN: 978-1-0369-0575-0

Published by Wisdom House Publishing
www.happyselfpublishing.com
writetous@happyselfpublishing.com

*If you are reading this book,
you are already making a difference*

'Whether you think you can or think you can't either way you're right.'

-Henry Ford

To my two teachers and angels Joseph Ezekiel Philip and Giuliana Marie, my muse and cornerstone Mariela, my dad, my mum, my brother, my sister and God. Your unconditional love, support, and compassionate feedback keep me going. Gracias de corazón.

Jose Enrique Gonzatti

To Karelin, Miranda and Maxima, the heart and pulse of my
life. Las amo hasta el infinito.

Javier Rosales

Acknowledgements

We would like to express our heartfelt gratitude to all the professionals in the world of coaching, positive change management, and book publishing who partnered with us to make this project a reality. A special mention goes to Sushmitha, Sunaina, Jyotsna, and the team at Happy Self-Publishing for their incredible support; to Victor Hugo Manzanilla for prefacing this work with wisdom and meaning; to George Ingils for his advice and Harold Parker for contributing to expanding our message in the digital world. To our coachees, some of whose stories are represented here, thank you for sharing glimpses of your journeys and passions for self-improvement, and for giving us the opportunity to learn and grow alongside you. Our deepest appreciation goes to our multiple coaches and role models, who have been beacons of serenity and self-improvement, often without even knowing it. To our parents and beloved wives, your continuous support has been a cornerstone of this endeavour. We also honour the memories of our friends who are no longer with us. To each one of you now reading these lines, you are a spark fuelling the fire in our hearts to make the Deliberate Coaching dream a reality. Finally, to each other —the quijotanos on a mission to create a world where everyone supports each other in finding their heart and taking action to achieve their goals, while building a compound and positive impact on all of society—thank you for your vision and dedication.

Table of Contents

Part 3

Foreword

Decades ago, I was hired as an intern at Procter & Gamble. This was my first job after college, and my first weeks were filled with fear and a profound feeling of impostor syndrome: Why me? Can I really bring any value?

I met amazing people during my first weeks in the internship, but one of them was special – Javier.

Javier Rosales was around my age, but he was managing a department of more than 20 people that was critical for the operation of the company. And I was an intern full of fears. I thought to myself: one day, I want to be like him. How can he, being so young, lead so well to all these people?

I remember he had a whiteboard next to his desk where he would write very thoughtful quotes so everyone in the department could see them. These were not superficial motivational one-liners but deep ones. I used to walk by, read them, and return to my desk to think about them.

In my first meeting with him, rather than sharing all his achievements and responsibilities, he showed great interest in me, my life, and my other endeavours.

He made me feel important. He made me feel like I could really add value. He gave his full, undivided attention to me during these 30 minutes. I left that meeting feeling more secure and appreciated. I knew he had something special.

Our career paths diverged after a few years, and I didn't see him again for almost 20 years.

I was so excited when we reconnected (and when I met his co-author José Enrique Gonzatti). The beauty of the internet made our paths cross again.

The social media algorithm connected us. During our careers, all of us developed a passion for coaching.

Coaching brought us together, and I was eager to know what Javier and Jose Enrique had learned and developed during the past decade.

That is this book.

We have seen an explosion of fake gurus and shallow motivators. Coaching has become a commodity, where anyone can call themselves a coach and build a following based on superficial, feel-good, one-minute videos.

We need a true transformation. We need people who lead real organisations, who truly need to coach people to deliver results, and who will come out and tell us how to do it.

These people are Javier and Jose Enrique: They are in the trenches daily, leading their teams to achieve exceptional results.

This book is a transformative journey into the heart of coaching, focusing on the powerful combination of intention, curiosity, and measurable results.

I have been stuck several times in my life. A ceiling that has kept me in a mediocre state of my life or my business, and coaching has been my key to progress: developing new skills, overcoming obstacles, and achieving my aspirations.

I've learned that happiness has some correlation with progress. In my most unhappy moments, including a profound period of depression, a coach helped me be aware of my situation, make peace with the unchangeable, and move towards the things that I had some influence on. That progress, even if small, took me back to the game.

I discovered something years ago: Every human being knows that they have more potential than the current results show. You can talk with people who are really struggling in life, and they will admit they have a lot of potential. You can talk with very successful people, and they will admit they have a lot of potential.

Our level of fulfilment (or happiness) is proportional to what we feel that gap is. But the truth is that we all have a gap between our potential and results.

Deliberate Coaching draws on this gap in human potential, harnessing the principles of curiosity and continuous improvement to create a dynamic and impactful coaching model. At its core, this book emphasises the importance of a learner's mindset – one that is open, inquisitive, and committed to growth. This mindset is the key to unlocking progress and achieving the desired results, whether in personal development, professional advancement, or any other area of life.

My advice: Start this book with a relentless commitment to growing. Whether you are a seasoned professional seeking to enhance your leadership skills, an athlete striving for peak performance, or someone simply looking to make positive changes in your personal life, this book offers valuable insights and practical tools to support your journey.

Maybe you will feel in love with not only with what coaching can do for you, but what you can do for others as a coach, and you may join our purpose. Time will tell.

As you delve into the chapters of this book, you will encounter compelling stories, practical examples, and insightful reflections that illustrate the transformative power of *Deliberate Coaching*. You will learn how coaching can create a positive ripple effect, impacting not only the individual coachee but also their communities, organisations, and beyond. The insights generated through coaching sessions provide valuable data that can drive broader changes and improvements, making coaching a vital tool for personal and collective growth.

In a world that is constantly evolving, the ability to adapt, learn, and grow is more crucial than ever. *Deliberate Coaching* offers a roadmap for navigating this journey with intention, clarity, and purpose. It invites you to embrace the principles of curiosity, resilience, and continuous improvement, empowering you to achieve your best self and make meaningful contributions to the world around you.

I am confident that as you read *Deliberate Coaching*, you will find inspiration, guidance, and practical strategies to support your journey of self-discovery and growth. You will close the gap. Whether you are new to coaching or an experienced practitioner, this book will deepen your understanding of the coaching process and enhance your ability to achieve transformative results.

Get comfortable, enjoy your journey of Deliberate Coaching – a journey that promises to close the gap between your potential and results, amplify your strengths, and guide you toward a future of limitless possibilities.

Victor Hugo Manzanilla
Bestselling author and CEO and Chairman of the Board of Salarius LTD, a startup developing low-sodium salt

Curiosity Eats Routine for Breakfast

A LIFE STORY – THE REALITY IS WHAT IT IS BUT HOW YOU APPROACH IT IS YOUR CHOICE

*I*t is early morning, the sun is rising, and you can hear birds chirping in the background. The first sense of awareness in your brain appears, and you realise it is a new day. The usual thoughts start to pop up; interestingly, your eyes are still shut. *What is on your mind? What are these thoughts popping up about? Most importantly, how are these making you feel? Do these feelings and thoughts have a recurring theme?*

Eventually, you open your eyes and before you know it, the phone is in your hand; you are scrolling away while also trying to read what seems like too many notifications, in the blink of an eye you are already late so you jump out of bed and get yourself in your full action mode, playing catch up with a long list of tasks before rushing out the door. Then, as you get to the bus stop, the bus shuts the door in your face and leaves, and you have to walk to the train station with the impeding thought of your day getting more difficult with each step. When you get on the train, a lady bumps into you and says nothing. Everyone is glued to the screens of their phones and with their headsets on, they all seem annoyed and zombie-like. You get to work already mentally drained, plough through the motions, and attend non-stop meetings where you feel you are barely making an impact. On top of that you aren't even able to make time to have lunch. There seem to be challenges and issues everywhere, and just like that, the day is gone. You have been really busy and are feeling completely exhausted, yet you can't but wonder, *"What have I actually accomplished?* You try to convince yourself with the narrative that, *It was a terrible day, but I did what I could from the things I had in front of me.* But inside your chest, there is a bubbling feeling that whispers *"failure"* and *"missed opportunity to become better."* As you experience it, you immediately shut it down. You pick up the phone to scroll the news or social media, as an unconscious brain reaction to attempt to put down the rebellion, and extinguish the burning sensation that something has to change. The heart is weakened after years of life routine and the same old patterns, motivation to try new things and change is just nowhere to be found. You keep scrolling until you fall asleep. You were busy, yet unfortunately, you did not get any closer to the goals you set for yourself at the beginning of the year. Another day goes by ... tomorrow – most likely – you will face another "rushed and busy" day.

Does this story:

- Represent a "day in your life"?
- Resonate with you on some level?
- Maybe this is not you, but you know someone who – from your perspective – seems to be experiencing this life right now or did at some point?

All the above options are invitations to reflect, empathise, visualise and broaden perspectives from the ways humans experience life. This is the essence of what a coach does. A coach listens actively, observes carefully, and finds the right questions to create an open dialogue that encourages reflection – sparks unlearning and rethinking – and leads to the coachee finding answers to deal with their day-to-day reality, to ultimately act to achieve results towards a desired goal.

Each human being is unique, and as they live their lives, individuals learn strategies and behaviours to deal with reality, sometimes by trial and error and survival instincts. During this process, people develop mindsets that govern how they see, perceive, and make decisions as they confront life situations.

Now, imagine an alternative version.

It is early in the morning; the sun is rising, and you can hear birds chirping in the background. The first sense of awareness in your brain appears, and you realise it is a new day. The usual thoughts start to pop up; interestingly, your eyes are still shut.

Then, you realise you can step back from the stampede of these thoughts. You find a space where you feel at peace, calm and in control, with the sense of "suspension in time and space", your mind in focus mode. You become mindful of this moment and take the driver's seat of your brain and body. Everything feels warm and quiet. You are not in reaction mode; on the contrary, you are in a position where you can deliberately embrace the full beauty and simplicity of this awakening for what it is – a new chance to live another day.

You then feel your heart beating in your chest, your lungs filling with air, and a joyful wave of gratitude rippling through your body. At the same time, you replenish yourself with compassion and kindness because you realise and accept that despite all that may be happening in your life right now, successes and failures, you are doing your absolute best, which is ok. Then, you think about what your heart most wants, perhaps an energiser word, a memory, or an image of someone. You feel a true and real connection with your inner self, and you stay there, breathing mindfully, on that moment until you exhale one long breath and open your eyes, you see your phone and grab it to check the time but pay little to no attention to any notifications before you put it down and get out of bed with a sense of courage and empowerment, and off you go to bravely face a new day.

Your list of activities awaits; you get ready to leave for work at your own pace. You are walking to the bus stop and see the bus there, but when you arrive, the bus driver closes the door and leaves. You laugh at it and think to yourself, *I was so close!* Then take this as the perfect opportunity to put some steps in; after all, you have been thinking about getting fitter for some months now, so this is an excellent opportunity to put thought into action. You arrive to the train platform and feel particularly focused and energised, catch your train, and use the commute time to reflect on that personal goal you thought about some months ago but have not managed to prioritise yet… *today is the day!* you think to yourself, and you feel a smile on your face.

As you get into the office, you say hello to Jasper, the receptionist. He is not usually friendly and sociable, but you have always addressed him with kindness, seen him for the person he is, and you suspect from his attitude towards you that he values and appreciates your attitude. He smiles at you and welcomes you. Then, you find a desk, attend your meetings for the day, and, through a curious and open mindset, manage the challenges and situations as they come along. Before you leave the office, you review your to-do list, plan for the next day, and head back home.

It has been a long day. You know it and accept it, and as you sit on the bus on the way back, you take stock of what went well today and what you could do better tomorrow. You get home, have dinner and take a hot bath to wind down after a long day. As you feel the water dropping, a sense of fulfilment fills your chest, and the "suspension in time and space" moment from this morning takes you over. You feel grateful; you know you have taken the lead of your life and journey, letting your curiosity drive your actions, and a step closer to your personal best. You have stretched and grown a bit, and tomorrow, this new and improved version of you will have another chance to make an impact and live another day.

Hopefully, this alternative perspective has poked your curious self. This is the mindset we invite you to embrace before reading this book – a curious mindset – one that allows for learning, as well as unlearning habits and behaviours that no longer serve you, pulling you away from routine and status quo and towards new possibilities. Curiosity is the key to change, to entertain the idea that everyone has the power to define, own and walk their journey regardless of any particular hat or role they may perform at any given point in their lives e.g. coach, coachee, teacher, doctor, cleaner, etc.

YOUR LIFE'S JOURNEY IS UNIQUE BUT NOT FIXED; SELF-AWARENESS AND WILLINGNESS TO CHANGE HOLDS THE KEY TO DISCOVERING ALTERNATIVE APPROACHES AND RESULTS.

On any given day, an individual will do what it takes to deal with life. The survival instinct and the person's self-awareness, understood as the conscious knowledge of one's own feelings and character, drives decision making and action. The former, due to its innate nature more difficult to control and manage, the latter, one that can we can potentially develop and that is intrinsically linked to our ability to continuously learn and grow beyond what we think is our fixed self at any given moment in time.

Being curious, challenging truths and beliefs, and then accepting that there is no such thing as static knowledge or "one truth", are few of many ways for someone to push their boundaries and improve their self-awareness. Heraclitus summarised it remarkably when he said, "Change is the only constant."

When we embrace change we unlock the door towards a world full of new alternatives and possibilities to trailblaze our life's journey, and if we add compassion and acceptance of ourselves – putting behind the chase for external validation but instead trusting and loving our identity for who we truly are in our hearts – we are then fully equipped to face with courage and confidence any peaks and valleys that we may find along the way as we walk toward achieving our goals and happiness.

Evolving as human beings to deal with life, aiming to achieve desires and goals, while also being true to ourselves, is certainly not an easy task. The allure of mirroring others' paths or strategies can be enticing. However, this inclination may lead us to regress to square one, as it disregards the fundamental truth that each individual is unique. What may appear as a successful journey from an external perspective is merely a subjective interpretation, and adopting it without discernment may not apply to one's distinct situation and circumstances. Trying out new approaches will always be positive and bring learnings and insights, especially those that have proven to generate results, but adapting them to your reality is key.

Introduction

$\mathcal{E}$nter Edgard-the-Pig, the youngest of the Three Little Pigs and the one who built the first house of straw blown away by the wolf. He tries to step away from the shadow of his oldest brother Bruce, who became a sensation after building the "brick house", and his middle brother William, a recognised surgeon. Edgard struggles to find his identity and to move away from the stigma and feeling of not being good enough for a successful life.

He eventually finds a career; however, it brings back past fears and makes his performance at work a continuous challenge. Embarking on his personal journey, he encounters a wise Owl Coach who becomes his guiding light through the maze of uncertainties. As he diligently seeks his true self and identity, he undergoes a profound transformation, reshaping not only his thoughts and behaviours but also refining his performance and delivery for Chelsea FC. Unveiling an unforeseen pig version of himself, he wholeheartedly embraces the essence of Deliberate Coaching at its best. You will find this entertaining.

This book is a journey of exploration on coaching, what it is, how it can transform lives for coaches, coachees, and everyone but most importantly a book written in a way so that you can take it in and make it yours, right and true to your life, and your circumstances. It is a quest to find clarity and focus in your mind – and your heart – so that you can compassionately accept yourself as a novice in the search for the answers that will lead to actions and changes in your life. It is our humble effort to impact others via socialisation of what we believe will have an everlasting change on everyone who tries coaching, a deliberate version of it, with the conviction and structure to achieve results.

In these pages, we will leverage data, experience-based insights, management science and stories as we walk you through our vision of how to make coaching accessible, delve into why coaching is important, and introduce you to the model that we trust will materialise this vision. The book is divided into three parts.

The first part describes the methodology fundamentals, including the importance of coaching, delivering results and combining both as the space where Deliberate Coaching best works, its constituents and how they interconnect to create effective coaching instances to define and shape the "Heart and Pulse" of the individual.

The second part is our flagship story, the tale of Edgard-the-Pig and the character at the start of this chapter. You will find a light-hearted but relevant contemporary narrative with familiar situations and characters from the professional world. The book is full of imagery, grounded in the principles of Deliberate Coaching from both the coach's and the coachee's perspectives.

The third part is the story within the story and explains the tale of Edgard-the-Pig and how it connects with the Deliberate Coaching methodology, bridging parts I and II. It dissects the main characters and plots concerning how the coaching journey unfolds when applied consistently to achieve a goal. It is full of spoilers, so make sure you read it only after the first two parts.

Human beings are unique. They are a complex mixture of hereditary traits, experienced events, social environmental factors and their own spark and genuineness, among many others. They do their best to live their lives and navigate challenges; nonetheless, many are unaware of how support from a coach can help find direction, clarity, and a compounded effect to achieve whichever objective and goal in their hearts.

This search for perspective and improvement is unique to you, but the journey is not one you need to do alone. Research (and experiences shared throughout this book) show that your chances of success – if accompanied by someone else – will multiply if you work with a coach.

However, it is not all plain sailing; there is no hack or magic trick in these pages to make anything happen without the hard work and commitment to consistently aim for your best – whatever "best" means for you. A curious mind is the first step on this journey. A curious mind constantly seeks to absorb new knowledge, expanding your thinking and perception of reality, potentially driving change in behaviours, and exploring new ways and results.

You bought this book. You are probably eager, excited and genuinely curious about what may lie ahead. You might also be thinking, am I a coachee, a coach, none, all? In practice it doesn't matter, since the chapters will cater for all, as long you have a curious mind. We hope you are already wondering which potential alternatives and possibilities are waiting for you at the other end.

We trust in your capacity to stay open as you read these pages, but most importantly, we are true believers that everyone should have access to support on their journey to achieve their personal best and feel seen, heard and valued. If you don't feel curious by now, if there is no itching or excitement to turn to the next page, that is fine. Maybe it is not your time yet which would have been the case for Edgard-the-Pig if he had given up... Well, you will read it for yourself!

Before you immerse yourself in exploration, we would like to leave you with two thoughts. Firstly, a big thank you for giving us – and yourself – the opportunity to learn together about Deliberate Coaching and improving performance, opening our minds to a life full of possibilities. Secondly, we offer you a chance to commit to leaving your ego and past beliefs behind and enjoy the read with a curious mind.

Enjoy your Deliberate Coaching journey!

PART 1

Coaching Is Important. It Can Be the Catalyst of Meaningful Life Changes

A LEARNER'S MINDSET HOLDS THE KEY TO PROGRESS.

A newborn baby cannot survive on its own and is completely dependent on an adult. The baby cannot take care of her basic needs without 24/7 support. She cannot feed itself, and cannot articulate words. It takes newborns at least the first two or three years of their lives – until they become toddlers – to start to communicate using short sentences, and to learn and label the feelings they experience daily, i.e. expressing hunger with words, rather than crying when they feel a rumbling tummy as they did when they were 6 months old.

On one hand, newborns come into this world with the advantage of having an unbiased brain ready to absorb and learn. On the other hand, they possess a dedicated supporting network – parents, family, or carers – that facilitates their development and growth. This network is fully committed to creating the "practice arena" with the conditions necessary for infants to progress through their developmental stages. It provides a safe environment for them to practice the key skills until they become operational and eventually master them.

This model from the early years can offer valuable insights that we can all bring to our present to keep us energised and in a continuous improvement path.

ALL HUMANS LEVERAGE CURIOSITY AS THEIR FIRST TOOL TO LEARN.

Consider the developmental process of walking. A healthy newborn baby has never used its muscles when, in their mother's womb, they float in amniotic fluid. As the pregnancy progresses and approaches full term, so does the physical development of organs, bones, muscles, circulatory system, etc. However, despite all muscles needed for walking being formed, most are undeveloped, never properly used, nor fully stretched yet.

It is not until the baby is finally out that the real world experience and the process of learning to move commences. First, they discover they can fully stretch, and then they spend the next months tossing, trying to turn, wiggling and moving. Eventually – at their own pace – the baby progresses and gradually develops muscle tone and strength to the point where they can sit unaided, keep their head high, and start to work on their balance, achieving results and progress milestones until they are able to explore on their own by pushing themselves up.

The infant is compelled to overcome challenges and frustrations, motivated by instincts, curiosity, and an inner voice propelling exploration. Simultaneously, there's a thirst for discovering objects and experiencing diverse sensations such as lights, shapes, and textures. This constant positive reinforcement to the brain fosters the formation of new connections.

These connection-forming processes happen while the caregiver is present, creating confidence and trust in the relationship.

SOMETIMES, YOU MOVE BACKWARDS AND SIDEWAYS BEFORE YOU CAN MOVE FORWARD.

As the infant begins the crawling journey – initially backwards, as upper body control and strength typically develop first – they gradually start looking up, attempting to climb and utilising objects for support. Through exploration attempts, they uncover a fresh perspective of the world, further motivating their attempts to stand and walk sideways, initially with assistance. After numerous failed attempts, trials, and errors, marked by remarkable resilience, the baby eventually takes a significant leap from the supportive furniture and ventures into the unknown to walk independently. The learning-to-walk process happens as a result of intuition, curiosity and sheer physical and mental effort. The human baby's body and brain learn to control their arm movement first, developing more strength and control on the upper body, making them push themselves backwards, until later when the lower body development catches up, and the combined motion kicks in, allowing them to finally push forward. Babies at this stage have no awareness of the art of the possible when it comes to moving, let alone that they will eventually move at will. It is instinct and curiosity at its purest form that drives them. However, as they continue to explore the world around them, the knowledge gathered via the lived experiences allows for development and progress. When achieving milestones, in this case, crawling and walking for the first time, their satisfaction and joy will be evident, and often, not only to the baby but also to those supporting them on the journey.

For the walking process, two important forces start to work together, which leads the baby to take the first steps, usually within 9 to 18 months. These are "the baby's force", fuelled by their intuition, curiosity, survival instinct and a large physical and mental effort, and "the supporter force", which provides the experience, physical and psychological safety, love and care, and continuous support from the caregiver. However, the latter serves as a catalyst to expedite the process, providing the baby with added momentum to attain the objective they might not achieve on their own. Babies are open, curious and fully focused on growing, learning and developing. At the same time, they feel the need and unconsciously accept any help and support from others on their journey towards development. Therefore, from a very early age, we are experiencing and leveraging others' help as we find our answers and achieve results on our growth path.

FORMAL COACHING ENABLES AND ACCELERATES THE GROWTH JOURNEY.

The definition of coaching is: "A partnership between a coach and a coachee, where the coach acts as an enabler to help the coachee achieve their personal best, and achieve their desired results in any area where they would like to see a change in their personal or professional lives". A coach prepares and trains using multiple techniques and gathers experience to master the necessary skills that drive the creation of the right environment for a coachee to navigate their journey in the search for their personal best. Coaches are individuals who feel passionate about learning about themselves yet intend to extrapolate and share with others the frameworks driving that self-awareness and discovery as a way to keep igniting their own and their coachee's inner fire.

A coach's sphere of influence encompasses a secure environment where individuals can freely express themselves without fearing judgement. It provides a practice arena for honing the skill of delving into hearts and minds. Additionally, it offers ongoing support, equipped with tools and frameworks, to facilitate the flourishing of ideas and the execution of actions towards predetermined goals. A coach acts as the sounding board and perfect companion on a coachee's discovery journey, one that sets the foundations for the first principle and insight. The coachee is in the driver's seat with his best "trusted advisor". The coach only facilitates – from the passenger seat – giving the coachee access to a toolkit of strategies and experiences that will help remove mental blocks and set them on the path to a new and better version that achieves their desired results.

The coach toolkit has many skills, mainly:

- Communication Skills (active listening)
- Human Relations Skills (empathy, supporting)
- Analytical Skills (questioning, providing feedback)

Through the practice and application of these skills, coaches improve people's chances of success, and they can apply this to any area of people's lives, personal, professional, sports, and academic, among others.

Let us use a corporate example and look at this anonymised case of a junior consultant with three years of experience who wanted to expand her professional boundaries and become a manager. Let's call her Mary, and her coach, George.

[Mary]: "Hi George, I have been in the company and this team for four months now. I enjoyed my onboarding, and although I am conscious of my learning curve, I came in with experience and want to become a manager."

[George]: "Thanks for sharing, Mary. It sounds like you want to leverage your previous experience to augment your impact on this team and expand your role to a manager role. Is that fair?"

[Mary]: "Exactly. I feel my previous teaching experience gives me great transferable skills that I am applying to my current role."

[George]: "Would you please tell me more?"

[Mary]: "Well, I have seen how much facilitation is needed in the clients' workshops and the interactions with some of our internal teams, like Legal and Operations. I was doing that with my students."

[George]: "If I understand correctly, it feels like you have already done some managing work, and this could be the stepping stone to embark on an acting manager role within the organisation."

[Mary]: "Exactly, a manager of others."

[George]: "Could you tell me what a manager of others means to you?"

[Mary]: "Mmmm…" She takes a moment to reflect on the question and then responds, "That is a good question. I think it means I get more freedom to lead some initiatives and make my own decisions."

[George]: (Repeats) "Freedom to lead and make my own decisions…"

There is a pause of about 10 seconds.

[Mary]: "Yes, freedom to lead and be accountable."

[George]: "Do you want to repeat that again with a bit more conviction?"

[Mary]: "I want freedom to lead and be accountable."

[George]: "Mary, this could be the name for your goal."

[Mary]: "It absolutely is!"

[George]: "Great progress, Mary. I am conscious of time, but I invite you to think about something before our next session. You have a key skill set in the facilitation space, but which skill set or skill sets do you think you need to further develop or start developing to be in a stronger position on your acting manager journey?"

[Mary]: (Mary acknowledges the question and starts to wonder and reflect for a few seconds, then responds) "Wow, I think I have some ideas, but let me take action to think about this properly. Thank you, George."

[George]: "Thank you, Mary, for sharing your thoughts and desires with me today. I am already energised by your 'freedom to lead' journey. Speak soon."

Coaching is built around asking rather than telling. To ask the right questions, a coach must listen actively (picking up as many verbal and non-verbal cues as possible), then apply key coaching skills and techniques to support a coachee – in this case, an aspiring manager – to create a safe environment where the coachee allows herself to be vulnerable and open, to explore her boundaries, develop self-awareness, and therefore, find within her the actions needed to aim for the best version of herself, and achieve her goal of becoming a manager. Most importantly, a good coach can unearth a core fibre that brings energy to the coachee that will allow not only for rapport and proximity going forward but also as a reminder of the goals that her heart desires.

In Mary's example, there is also evidence of the importance of the chemistry between coach and coachee. This is something that can be easily overlooked on the basis that coach training and skills are assumed to be transferable, yet they are ultimately founded on human interactions.

COACHING IS NOT JUST ABOUT SPORTS, IT CAN BE APPLIED TO MULTIPLE AREAS OF PEOPLE'S LIVES TO DRIVE THE DISCOVERY AND ACHIEVEMENT OF UNTAPPED POTENTIAL.

Coaching helps people find clarity on their objectives and consistently identify the actions to achieve these goals. There are multiple examples of how coaching has positively impacted a coachee's ability to improve their performance in both their professional and personal aspects.

There is also a clear example that tends to be top of mind to many people: sports coaching. A coach is always there to guide a team or an individual to improve their performance, individually and collectively. This is found across many sports, and people have either experienced this type of coaching at some point in their lives or seen it occur when watching any professional sports competition or when taking their children to sports lessons. People sometimes don't know that coaching is much more than "sports coaching", and if they were to take a coach to help improve their performance, it would not be someone shouting from the pitch sidelines and telling them to go to one place or the other.

A performance coach's journey unfolds beyond the conventional starting point; it begins with placing the coachee at the core, attentively tuning in to the fundamentals and unravelling the intricate tapestry of reality. This process culminates in skilful reflection, channelling the essence of what transpires and skilfully echoing back the poignant questions or statements that evoke resonance, ultimately revealing profound insights and inspiring decisive actions. The performance coach serves as the coachee's "support team", helping them recognise their boundaries and limits. The coach encourages the coachee to surpass these constraints in order to attain their optimal self on the journey toward achieving their desired goal.

Eliud Kipchoge, the Kenyan long-distance runner who is regarded as the greatest marathon runner of all time, has managed not only to work tirelessly to do everything in his power but also build an inner circle of support to allow him to push his boundaries and improve his results to its maximum each time. Eliud explains this philosophy of team collaboration for maximum results in this way: "You cannot train alone and expect to run a fast time. There's a formula. 100% of me is nothing compared to 1% of the whole team."

A PROBLEM SHARED IS A PROBLEM HALVED.

It is common to see individuals attempting to navigate day-to-day challenges independently. Yet, their thinking in some situations may be biased by their principles, experiences, and beliefs, which could hinder creativity and innovation in dealing with problems and reinforcing existing patterns and behaviours.

Working with a coach brings a new lens to explore new perspectives towards desired outcomes. In a safe environment there is trust in the relationship, and as the coachee allows himself to be vulnerable and share his desires, limitations also surface. The coach supports reframing the limitations, bringing the focus back into reality, and pivoting into finding viable options to get back on track to achieve goals. Sharing and exploring doubts around principles and situations brings a "discovery and curiosity mode".

LIFE IS CONSTANTLY CHANGING. EVERYONE CAN BECOME BETTER AT EMBRACING CHANGE AND TRANSFORM ANY ASPECT OF THEIR LIVES WITH THE SUPPORT OF A COACH.

Making a conscious decision to embark on a coaching journey opens the floodgates of imagination, creation and change. A sustainable change will turn into incremental and consistent results and victories, reinforcing the growth and curiosity mindset that does so much for humans when they are babies but unfortunately ends up losing traction and strength as life goes on. People start to take things for granted, prioritising security and less uncertainty over rist taking and being open to learning, probably due to fear of losing what has already been achieved.

The cumulative impact of the coachee's deliberate actions, coupled with their open mindset and unwavering commitment to the coaching process, combined with effective techniques, the conducive space and rapport established, and the forthcoming insights yet to be unearthed on the coaching journey, renders the whole experience both timeless and boundless. This multifaceted approach significantly amplifies the coachee's likelihood of success in their quest to realise their "best version", surpassing what they might have accomplished independently.

Coaching is a growth accelerator

KEY LEARNING POINTS:

1. All human beings have the potential to learn and improve their performance in any area of their lives.

2. Approaching learning with an open and curiosity mindset – like babies do when they start to walk – is the first step to increasing your ability to achieve success on desired goals.

3. A coaching partnership, that brings together external support from a coach to a motivated coachee, creates a safe space where experience, knowledge and coaching skills boost the coachee's chances to accelerate their growth journey.

4. Coaching applies to all fields and areas of life; it is universal, and everyone can benefit from engaging in a coaching relationship to improve and achieve whichever objective they have in their minds.

5. Life is constantly changing, and everyone has a curious instinct to deal with the changes. However, people's ability to adapt to change in a way that works best for them exponentially improves when receiving external support from a coach.

1. What is a memory from childhood – or earlier in your life – that you have where you used curiosity as a tool to learn to do something?

   ....

   ....

2. When did you last take ten minutes to sit and reflect on what you are looking for at this moment in your life? Allow yourself to do this now and come up with one dream/goal.

   ....

   ....

3. List three things that are holding you back from achieving your goal.

   ....

   ....

4. If you wanted to be (or already are) a coach or a coachee, what could be a thing to explore and action to take that you haven't tried before?

   ....

   ....

5. Can you think of an occasion when you were talking to someone and genuinely listening trying to learn more about this person situation or story rather than giving them your opinion and suggested solutions? What was this conversation about, how did you feel afterwards?

   ....

   ....

Coaching Is Transformational; However, not an Intuitive or Organic Life Choice, Yet

Business Coaching in the US alone generated \$14.1bn in annual revenue in 2023, driving 110K direct employees, and it was the core focus of over 70K companies, according to the IBIS World.[1] It relies heavily on reputation. Professional Development Training represents half of that potential, which reaches mainly middle and senior management personnel of US corporations. The sector grows as economic conditions fluctuate since companies seek coaches to navigate new business environments and current social issues, develop their business skills and enhance market competitiveness. In contrast, coachees (jobseekers, new managers) seek these services to become more competitive in the labour market.

---

1 Business Coaching in the US, Industry report. October 2023

It is also a resilient sector, proved by the dynamics observed during the recent COVID-19 pandemic, where coaches continued their work despite physical restrictions thanks to technology and the virtual connectivity tools available.

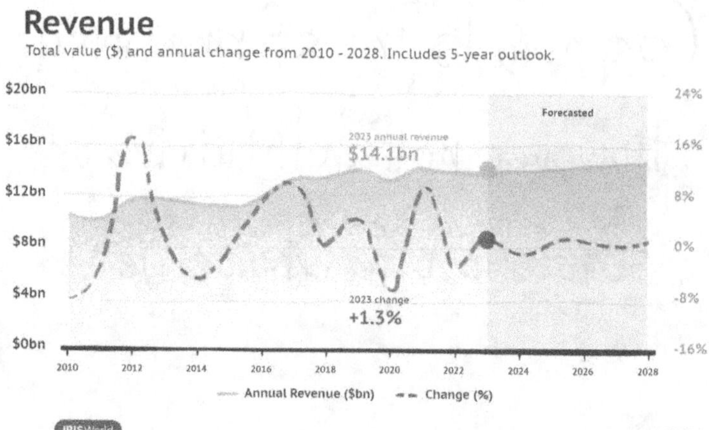

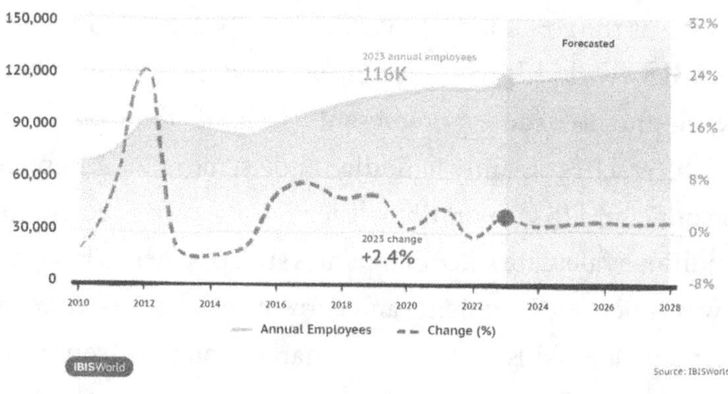

If this is extrapolated to the rest of the world, we can see a sizeable, addressable market where the conditions exist for coaching to thrive. However, we believe this picture could be even larger when we step away from business and corporates as the entities that conceive and deploy coaching programmes, and look at individuals eager to transform an aspect of their lives, regardless of having company support.

COACHING INCREASES A COACHEE'S ABILITY TO PROGRESS TOWARDS A BETTER VERSION OF THEMSELVES, SO WHY IS NOT EVERYONE DOING IT?

Despite the continuously growing base of certified coaches and the extensive benefits of working with a coach, as alluded to in the previous chapter, the practice is far from the norm at an individual and corporate level.

On the positive side, awareness and availability of the approach and its benefits have improved over the last decades; recognised training and accreditations have grown wider, and the stigma of engaging with self-help professionals has dramatically decreased with the advent of mental health and well-being awareness. Nonetheless, the percentage of the population within age brackets where they could aspire to work with a coach at a professional or personal level (i.e. 16 and above) is quite low and reflects a very nascent stage of maturity. A global coaching study commissioned by the International Coaching Federation (ICF), and published in 2023, brings insights into the client population:

- A little over one in two coach practitioners said their clients are mostly managers (31%) or executives (25%) – an increase of 4% versus 2019.

- On average, coach practitioners said that 57% of their clients are sponsored, and 43% are primary clients. Compared to 2019, the sponsored share has increased (up from 52%) while the primary share has fallen (48%).
- The majority of coaching clients (58%) are female. Compared with 2019, the average female share of clients has not changed significantly (57% in 2019).
- Clients aged between 35 and 44 years (37%) frequently receive coaching services, followed by clients in the 45 to 54 age range (32%). Around one in five (21%) are under 35 years old.

In spite of the steady engagement, we believe the potential to reach and support an important part of the professional population is large, yet would require removing detractors and limiting thoughts. Some of the most common are:

- Overconfidence in the ability to change and develop and to maintain that change in time.
- Lack of clarity on the coaching process and dynamics, i.e. misunderstanding the principles and workings of a coaching relationship and goals.
- Doubt and scepticism on the coach's credentials, academic and work experience being sufficient and adequate to support a change journey.
- Underrated or misunderstood from a value-for-money perspective.
- Stigma prevents seeking external support from a professional, i.e. misconception of having something

> wrong that requires fixing from – in this case – a coach.

- Association between coaching being a never-ending cycle of sessions without a clean cut and clear unit of measure to quantify progress, and no defined objective.

There is an opportunity to make coaching universal regardless of geography, culture, gender, age, religion, etc. It starts via a new coaching proposition that allows to tackle the unique journey of a coachee in any area of their choosing. Then, it creates a safe space that propels them forward, builds momentum at the right pace, drives action and insights whilst providing and leveraging quantifiable results to show progress. This, in turn, feeds the momentum and acts as a catalyst for success. We firmly believe that most perceived detractors can be overcome, especially those related to the ambiguous number of sessions or clarity on goals and ways to track progress towards them. We have seen that allowing for goal definition early on the journey, as the engine for actions and results, has positively impacted a coachee's ability to navigate their journeys, commit to the sessions, and adopt a courageous and consistent attitude throughout the coaching journey.

If you have read until here, we will assume that coaching has a place in your mental models; at worst, it is curiosity, and at best, it is conviction. You could then be in one of the four groups below:

1. **The Uninitiated Potentials** (Unknown Unknowns) – You don't know your potential and the real opportunity to improve, and constantly deal with life challenges and opportunities within your comfort zone and limitations.

2. **The Aware and Ready to Change** (Neutral Known Unknowns) – You know your limitations to reach your potential; you haven't tried coaching and are curious (or at least unbiased) towards it.

3. **The Jumper Sceptics** (Demoter Known Unknowns) – You know your limitations to reach your potential; you have tried some type of coaching but have not gathered a positive result or experience from it.

4. **The Coaching Allies** (Promoter Known Unknowns) – You are aware of your limitations to reach your potential

and are willing and eager to leverage coaching as a way to grow out of them. You have tried coaching, seen positive and tangible results, and will continue doing so.

Let us look at each of these groups while we meet some new characters.

Simon is a first-year university medical student. He is 18 years old, single and fully dedicated to his studies. He is a very smart and energetic guy, easygoing and passionate about helping others, which is the main driver for his going to med school as his career choice.

Simon's curiosity drives him towards learning, connecting and experiencing everything he can get his hands on. However, he sometimes struggles with focus and attention. He is not aware of this challenge, with attention being something he could get better at, and not aware of coaching as a way to improve his ability to be more consistent and to remove his fear of failure, which on occasion blocks his ability to move forward. There is a lot of untapped potential to find new ways to navigate his journey to achieve his goal of helping and supporting others, including pursuing other professional careers if the realisation of helping others is not necessarily strictly attached to a particular profession.

Insights around coaching adoption for this group: Lack of awareness regarding coaching as a means to strive for and attain superior results, coupled with blind spots hindering the recognition of untapped capacities and unrealised potential for improvement.

Esme is married with four children, has a finance degree, and works part-time for a nonprofit organisation (NPO). She is fully committed to being present and supporting her children while she finds meaning at work as the finance director of an NPO. She is organised and resourceful; however, now that her youngest is approaching the end of primary school, she thinks she is ready for a new challenge and potentially going back to full-time employment. Esme feels at a crossroads and in doubt about whether this is the right decision or why she thinks she should do this. After all, she manages everything very well with things as they are. She is self-aware of her limitations and, therefore, starts researching coaching and reaching out to an acquaintance who has used coaching for views and insights.

Insights around coaching adoption for this group: Awareness of coaching and its benefits / Willingness to explore as a way to gather clarity on goal and actions to achieve it / High self-awareness on strengths and improvement opportunities / Desire to improve with additional support than her own thinking and ways.

3. The Jumper Sceptics (Demoter Known Unknowns)

James is married at 28 years old and has no children. He is an ambitious and smooth operator, keen to move up fast on the corporate ladder. He started working at a well-known investment bank straight after university four years ago. He is a very well-qualified and thorough senior business analyst who feels prepared to take a managerial role. He has been so focused on building depth on his subject matter expertise that he has been unable understand the additional skills that a managerial role would require. He has received feedback over the last year from his line manager and other colleagues, but he has not acted on this as he prioritised his own perspective that becoming the best Senior Business Analyst is the only way to become a manager. James was put into a coaching programme last year to help build his journey towards management. However, after a handful of sessions, frequencies started to slip, and the cycle came to an end. He has not picked these up again since.

Insights around coaching adoption for this group: Preconceptions around success and how to achieve it. Low self-awareness around skills needed for goals. (Missing managerial skills are not on his radar, and not understood by James.) Coaching results from a previous experience are pulling him away from trying it again. He desires to improve but sees his methods and perspective as the way to improve current performance and step up to new challenges.

4. The Coaching Allies (Promoter Known Unknowns)

Micaela is a seasoned lawyer who has devoted her whole life to her career and has worked at her own legal practice for the last 20 years following a 15-year stint at a well-known legal firm where she started as counsel after university and worked her way up to partner. She had her first taste of coaching as part of her leadership preparation to become a partner, and based on the positive experience and results achieved, she decided to continue to work with a coach on other occasions – with similar positive outcomes – on life events. For example, she found coaching effective when she faced coming back to work after each one of her pregnancies, deciding on setting up her own legal practice and looking for guidance on how best to deal with behavioural issues with her eldest son, a teenager dealing with anxiety.

Insights around coaching adoption for this group: Clear and proven track record of results and success using coaching as an enabler / High level of self-awareness, confidence and flexibility to adapt to change and receive feedback.

DESPITE DIFFERENT LIFE EXPERIENCES, THERE IS A COMMON STARTING PLACE FOR THE COACHING JOURNEY.

Regardless of the group you identified to belong to, the place you live and the reality you deal with daily, you surely share a degree of curiosity and willingness to become better and drive change in one – or multiple – areas of life. People share a desire to be heard and seen, and coaching speaks to this need to connect, whilst it adds value to also providing new perspectives that feed the curiosity to learn, become better and achieve goals.

Chapter II Wrap-Up:

On the rise, with potential, yet work to do

KEY LEARNING POINTS:

1. The business coaching sector projects further opportunities to grow as the foundations set up over the last few years continue to answer both companies' challenges (e.g., new business environments) and coachees looking to adapt to market changes.
2. Research shows considerable untapped potential to further slice the large population that would benefit from a coaching relationship, not only at a corporate level (sponsored on occasions) but also at an individual level.
3. There has been progress towards tearing down walls around identified clear detractors to take on a coach, such as lack of clarity on the process, scepticism around credentials, stigma around looking for external support, etc., but there is some way to go.
4. Regardless of the four target groups we have identified, we believe there is an opportunity to make coaching universal, given its raison d'être, which is to support human beings in finding perspective to make decisions towards the achievement of a desired goal.

LEARNERS' CURIOSITY REFLECTION QUESTIONS:

1. Is there anyone in your close circle (family and friends) who has embarked on a coaching relationship? If so, would you feel courageous enough to ask them to share their experience with you? Write here the question or sentence you would use to approach them on this topic.

....

....

....

....

2. Have you ever worked with a coach? How was it? Write down two things that worked and two things that didn't. If you have never done it, write down two reasons why you think you should do it now and two things that are pushing you away from trying.

....

....

....

....

CHAPTER III

Impact and Tangible Results Boost Confidence and Are Important Ingredients for Sustainable Change

*I*t should come as no surprise that delivering results positively affects organisations, communities, teams, and, most importantly, individuals. From a neurochemistry perspective, achieving results can release dopamine, unleashing feelings of enjoyment and simultaneously reducing levels of cortisol (a hormone linked to stress and reactive behaviour). It ultimately boosts self-confidence and helps to build trust.

Each individual possesses the inherent potential for improvement and often harbours instances of successfully attaining results aligned with significant personal objectives.

You can pause for a moment, even close the book and remember an experience where you achieved something important to you, no matter how big or small, just something you put effort into, and remember how you felt when you achieved that result. It is very likely words like happy, fulfilled, and satisfied will start to come to mind. This sense of satisfaction would fuel and prime your brain to keep looking for further challenges to achieve.

At the same time, we know that achievement doesn't come "for free" and usually requires hard work, some external conditions, and even luck. It also strongly depends on the expectations and objectives against which the result will be measured. Setting goals, planning to achieve them, executing the plan – and adjusting them when needed – to reap results is a winning formula worth trying.

Small, measurable, yet continuous results can have a compounded positive effect that outweighs the more linear, *work long, hard and expect breakthroughs at the end approach*. Software Development approach "Agile" captures this mindset very accurately, as included in their Manifesto for Agile Software Development:[2]

> *"We are uncovering better ways of developing software by doing it and helping others do it. Through this work we have come to value:*
> - *Individuals and interactions over processes and tools*
> - *Working software over comprehensive documentation*

---

2 https://agilemanifesto.org/

- *Customer collaboration over contract negotiation*
- *Responding to change over following a plan*

That is, while there is value in the items on the right, we value the items on the left more."

Agile Values

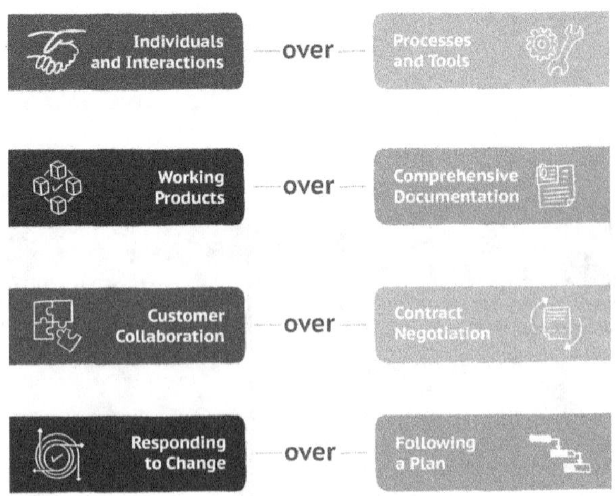

With Agile, projects are decomposed into milestones, so the iterative value can be delivered as these milestones are achieved, and risks are spread throughout, instead of them accumulating until a unique and final large result is achieved. It's the analogy of building and delivering a scooter first while continuing with the bicycle, motorcycle and finally, the car, as opposed to only focusing on delivering the latter.

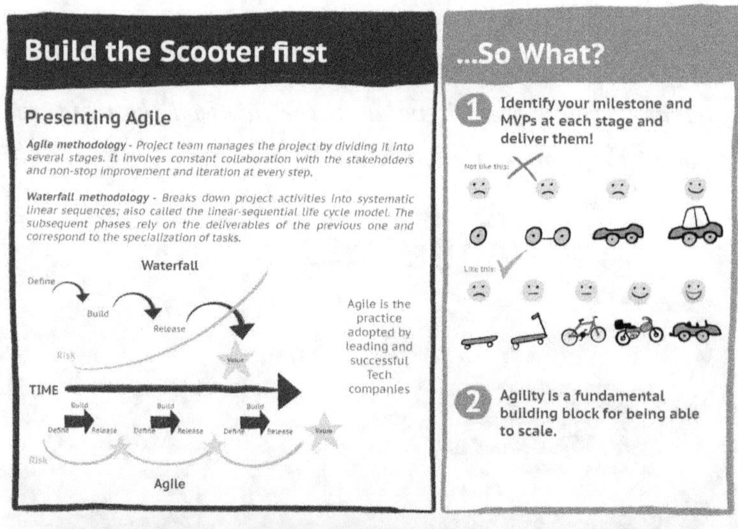

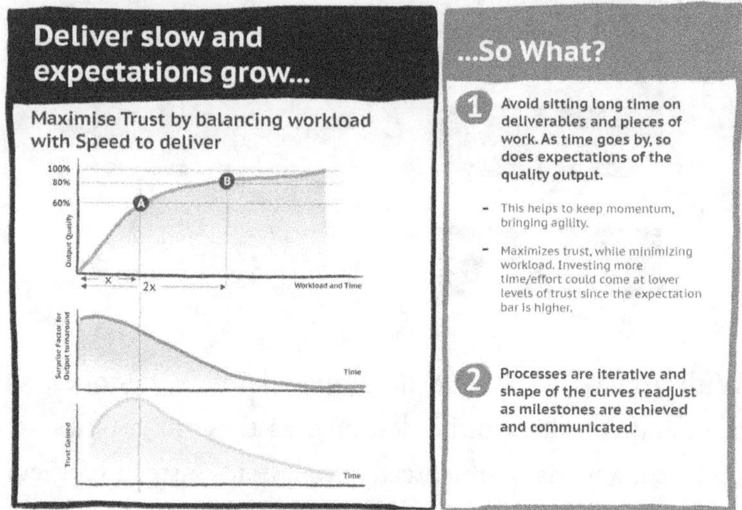

In addition to spreading out the product into pieces, speed matters. Trust is maximised when we are able to deliver a semi-complete result in a brief period of time, rather than a fully complete sroduct in a much longer period (by when the urgency or excitement might have faded).

Achievement of goals has a major positive impact on people's lives, and it also has a ripple effect on other areas of their personal and professional lives. When done properly – and by trained and experienced professionals – coaching creates the right environment and helps a coachee find their pace towards a virtuous cycle that lands in achieving the coachee's personal best. The implication for our story is that coaching journeys can become more effective and transformational if they are accompanied by a framework to deliver results in the agile way, and that is, in essence, **a Deliberate Coaching Journey**.

Chapter III Wrap-Up:

Results make long-term satisfaction

KEY LEARNING POINTS:

1. A disciplined approach and principles to drive small, measurable, and continuous results – as the software development "Agile" approach – is one that, if extrapolated to a coaching business model, could bring a compounded effect towards the coachee's success.

2. By decomposing and breaking down dreams/goals into milestones and actions, iterative value can be achieved over a set period of time.

3. Milestone achievements – considered and perceived as small successes – become the stepping stone to training and improving a coachee's ability to develop the skillset and mindset needed to achieve the ultimate goal.

LEARNERS' CURIOSITY REFLECTION QUESTIONS:

1. Remember a recent achievement. How did you feel when you first registered the completion? How do you feel now looking back?

2. Now think of a recent failure. What did you learn from it? What would you differently next time?

Introducing Deliberate Coaching: The Transformational Power of Coaching Meets the Positivity of Delivering Results

Harnessing the transformational power of coaching to deliver meaningful and tangible results lies at the centre of our proposition. The elements that define it can be summarised using a human body analogy:

1. **The Brain, the body of knowledge,** brings the concept of this methodology to life. This book, as well as the derived articles and coverage, practices, and pieces of insights available, are part of it. Bringing the analogy to our beloved organ, it's not static, rather it learns and is

able to incorporate new information and insights and improve the discipline itself.

2. **The Heart (and Pulse), the methodology** at the centre of our proposition, is how coaches and learners interact, generating learnings and tangible results. In analogy with our own heart, it sets the pace and rhythm and gives life to the entire system where both learners and coaches materially benefit.

3. **The Arms and Legs, the learners' and coaches' experiences** include details of the advances by these two groups, where goals are achieved, and improvements registered (learners) and new professional milestone and compensation (or rewards) obtained (coaches). They provide the speed and strength of our proposition and the ability to keep innovating and delivering value.

4. **The Voice, the insights generator,** codifies a large number of data points from a large number of coaching instances and transforms them into images (insights) that could be used to draw attention to patterns and engage external parties to act. This entity would provide the ability to grow and drive meaningful changes at scale since we could empower other bodies with the resources to support talent development programmes.

We expect a symbiotic relationship across all these components that will create a virtuous cycle (positive flywheel). We will analyse each of these in the subsequent sections.

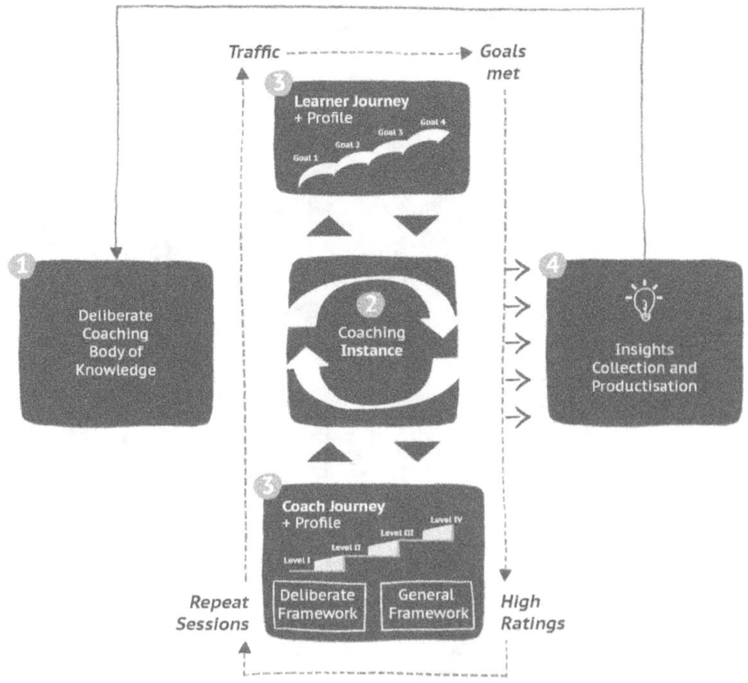

(1) THE BRAIN: THE DELIBERATE COACHING DISCIPLINE AND ITS STRATEGIC POSITIONING

In chapters 1 and 2, we discussed coaching as a discipline and showcased its potential to materially transform lives and mindsets. In this chapter, we want to set the context and place coaching together with other transformational tools (like therapy or counselling) and go deeper into the different ways that coaching can be used to arrive at the main point of this book – a coaching that is intentional, with a goal in mind, consequential, most precisely, *Deliberate*.

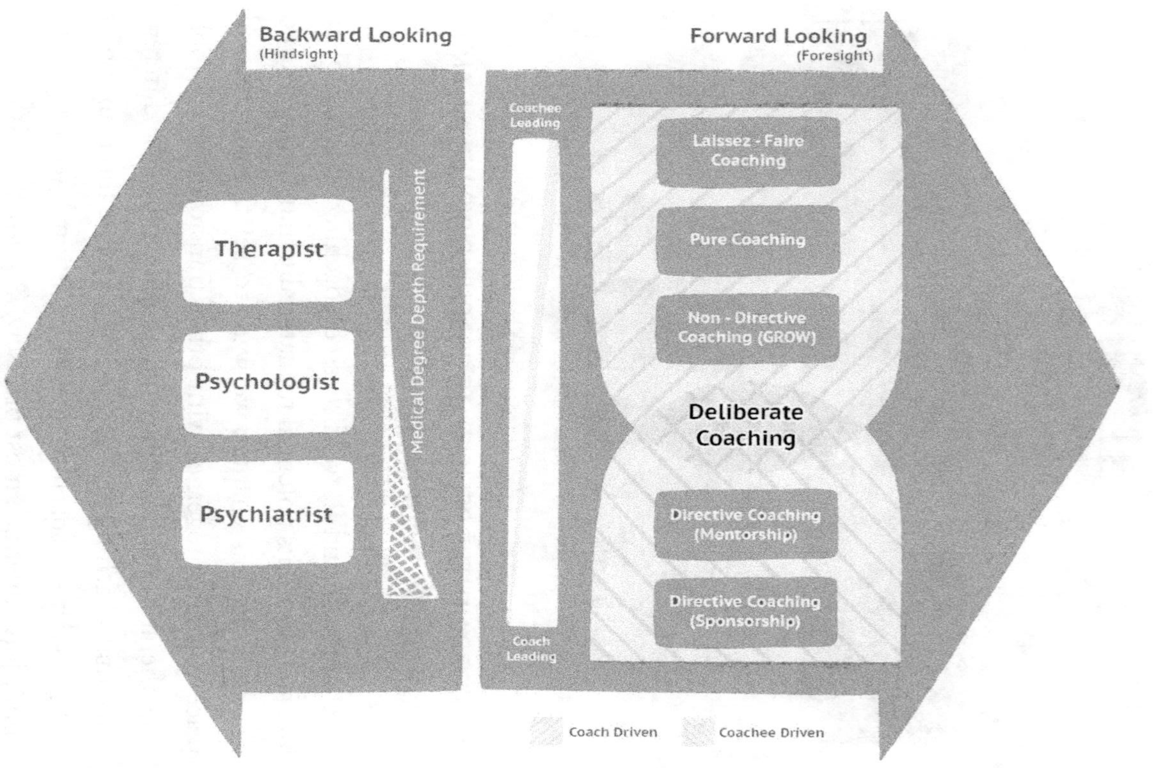
Backward Looking
(Hindsight)
Forward Looking
(Foresight)
Coachee Leading
Laissez - Faire Coaching
Pure Coaching
Non - Directive Coaching (GROW)
Therapist
Deliberate Coaching
Medical Degree Depth Requirement
Psychologist
Directive Coaching (Mentorship)
Psychiatrist
Directive Coaching (Sponsorship)
Coach Leading
Coach Driven
Coachee Driven

BACKWARD-LOOKING: COUNSELLING

Counselling is a term commonly associated with coaching as a potential option when some level of help or support is needed. At a very general level, they both involve the party interested in improving, usually an individual (but this could be extended to couples or groups) engaging in a conversational dynamic with a professional through a number of sessions. Still, there is a key difference: the direction of the focus.

Counselling places the problem at the centre, and in order to connect the person with possible solutions, it explores feelings, emotions and general behaviours that this problem triggers, and tries to look back to understand the causes. Professionals explore personal spaces which could include relationships, childhood, feelings, emotions, thoughts, past and present life events and situations or difficulties. In summary, it looks at the underlying context over which the current problem emerged, aiming to bring awareness and define a plan to work on these elements.

Even in this space, there are three levels: therapists, psychologists and psychiatrists.

The British Association of Counselling Professionals (BACP) states, "*Therapy provides a safe and confidential space for you to talk to a trained professional about your issues and concerns. Your therapist will help you explore your thoughts, feelings and behaviours so you can develop a better understanding of yourself and of others. A counsellor will not give you their opinions or advice or prescribe medication. They will help you find your own solutions – whether that's making effective changes in your life or finding ways of coping with your problem."*[3]

Therapists provide mental health diagnoses and develop a treatment plan. They are licenced professional counsellors, in most cases requiring a master's degree and approval of their licensing boards to practice in the mental health field.[4]

Psychologists are also mental health professionals who specialise in studying behaviours and mental processes, including cognitive and emotional processes and how people interact with their environment and others. They can diagnose and treat mental disorders, learning disabilities and behavioural problems (including supporting stressful events, addictions or illness. Practising psychologists must have an undergraduate major, a master's, and a doctorate in psychology.[5]

Psychiatrists are medical doctors. "Like psychologists, psychiatrists specialise in the study, diagnosis, prevention, and treatment of emotional, mental, behavioural, and developmental issues. Psychiatrists diagnose mental disorders and focus on chemical imbalances in the brain. They can assess both the mental and physical effects of a disorder. However, unlike psychologists, psychiatrists are medical doctors, or physicians, with a degree in medicine."[6]

---

3 https://www.bacp.co.uk/about-therapy/what-is-counselling/

4 https://www.mana.md/psychologist-psychiatrist-or-therapist/

5 https://www.mana.md/psychologist-psychiatrist-or-therapist/

6 https://www.mana.md/psychologist-psychiatrist-or-therapist/

Psychiatrists must complete an undergraduate and medical degree, plus a residency in psychiatry.

FORWARD-LOOKING AND NON-DIRECTIVE WITH THE ATTENTION ON THE COACHEE

We stated that counselling explores the individual's environment and the problem and looks back to the causes. Coaching looks to reframe the problem to an area of importance and explores and deep dives into the hypothetical future where this milestone has been achieved.

As in counselling, there are several degrees in which the interrelation between the coach and the coachee can happen. The first group has the coachee at the centre and covers three types: Laissez-faire, Pure Coaching and GROW Coaching.

We will explore them and learn from the case of Bob, a recently promoted manager in a technology company who aims to be selected to drive the strategic review of the business unit by the end of the year. Bob will work with Coach Alice.

LAISSEZ FAIRE (HANDS-OFF, HOLISTIC OR DELEGATIVE) COACHING

In this approach, the coachee is free to pursue their development in any direction, with limited or no structure. Conversations can take different directions and turns and explore as many or as few topics as possible, following the learner's discretion. The coach removes his authority from the engagement.

It assumes implicitly that the conversation space is enough to benefit the coachee, that there is comfort with the learner making mistakes or that there is no time expectation to achieve improvements.

When this approach is transferred to Leadership Styles, one example frequently mentioned is The CEO of Berkshire Hathaway Inc., Warren Buffet, who focuses on hiring top talent to give them autonomy in decision-making, encouraging them to go above and beyond the boundaries of their role descriptions.

Bringing this to a Bob and Alice session:

[Bob] "I have just been promoted to People Manager, and have a team of six. I haven't managed anyone before and I am used to working on things on my own. I understand this is important for my career progression, so I took the opportunity without hesitation. But I find that I don't know what to change or how to even start."

[Alice] "Okay, that's interesting. What are you doing at the moment about it?"

[Bob] "Well, I set a weekly team meeting and shared the team's goals. I offered help when they needed it and shared how excited I was to have them on the team."

[Alice] "Do you think this worked?"

[Bob] "It's difficult to say. They all nodded and agreed on the plan but didn't say much after."

[Alice] "What will you do next?"

[Bob] "I will have 1:1s and individual reviews to understand where they individually sit and how worried I should be."

[Alice] "And after?"

[Bob] I haven't thought that far ahead. I guess I will leave it a few weeks and see how the dynamics unfold."

[Alice] "Okay, let's connect again when that happens."

PURE/CLEAN COACHING

This type of coaching aims to build the "purest or cleanest" coaching experience possible for the coachee. To do this, the coach focuses on clean language, keeping the coachee's keywords as much as possible, and reflecting these back verbatim to create a seamless thinking and reflecting process that produces proximity and safety for the coachee. This coaching method also searches for targeted questions that leverage keywords, or the coachee's input, into a form that removes pressure on the coachee by removing presuppositions, e.g. instead of asking, "What are you thinking?" then asking, "Is there anything else about…?"

Pure/clean coaching requires trust from the coach whilst also being mindful and fully present for the coachee to select the keywords (or phrases) on the spot, and use them to go along with it. It is a balancing act, and one that requires practice, as the coach should capture hints in real time (words, movement, pauses, etc.) and decide on how to play this back to the coachee, i.e. whether to repeat the keyword and leave a pause for the coachee to reflect, or to make the keyword part of a targeted question back to the coachee, etc.

Bringing this to a Bob and Alice session:

[Bob] "I have just been promoted to People Manager, and have a team of six. I haven't managed anyone before and am used to working on things on my own. I understand this is important for my career progression, so I took the opportunity without hesitation, but now I find that I do not know what to change or how to even start!"

[Alice] "Thanks for sharing, Bob. I heard you say you took the opportunity without hesitation, correct?"

[Bob] "Yes, exactly. I have been waiting for an opportunity to help others grow as I expand and grow myself."

[Alice] "Expand and grow..."

[Bob] "Expand to think differently and work alongside others as I am conscious that unlearning some habits is the only way to grow in my career journey."

[Alice] "Interesting, Bob. Do you have a particular habit you would like to focus on first in this new people manager role to help you start with an expanded and growing mindset?"

[Bob] "One comes to mind: setting up daily huddles with the team to build an open channel between them and me – an open door learning together approach."

[Alice] "What do you want to achieve with this open door learning together approach?"

[Bob] "The confidence that I am doing my best to support their growth as I grow myself into this people manager role."

[Alice] "Great stuff, Bob. I look forward to hearing how it is progressing with your team on our next connect."

GROW (OR SITUATIONAL) COACHING

This type of coaching was conceptualised in the mid 80s by Sir John Whitmore with the GROW (Goal, Reality, Obstacles, Options, Will) model, which unlocks values by driving insights and learnings across four areas:

1. Goal. At the front and centre of the coaching engagement, it defines the problem and articulates how success will be measured and understood by the learner. Goals should be established from a place of excitement and enthusiasm to increase the chances of success. A common framework to define goals is for them to be EXACT:
   Explicit. Only one focus, using a few words
   Xciting. They should be exciting and positively framed
   Assessable. Goals should be measurable
   Challenging. Stretching, yet within reach
   Time Framed. Ideally within 3-6 months

2. Reality. This is the space to explore the context, the "what is happening right now?" covering what, when, where

and who, starting from the general and letting the learner complete the details.

3. Options. In this step, the coach frames the questions to generate alternatives to the solution beyond the ones initially brought by the learner (if at all). It is important to remove binary thinking and push to go beyond the obvious constraints (i.e. "Imagine you have a magic wand and remove the blockers, what then?")

4. Will. This is where the coach looks for the learner to affirm the next steps and define concrete actions to be taken. They should be small but meaningful and in the direction of the goal previously established.

In GROW coaching, coaches avoid inserting their personal opinions. Instead, they skillfully utilise targeted questions, most of which are open-ended, to facilitate the emergence of insights and the formulation of solutions by the learner. This coaching method is non-directive, yet it incorporates a structured and linear flow to guide the process effectively. A Bob-Alice session would be like this:

[Bob] "I have just been promoted to People Manager, and have a team of six. I haven't managed anyone before and am used to working on things on my own. I understand this is important for my career progression, so I took the opportunity without hesitation, but I now find that I don't know what to change or how to even start."

[Alice] "Why is this important for you?"

[Bob] "Well, I want to be able to lead a large unit someday. I want to have the opportunity to change things in a meaningful way and have a larger impact, and for that you need to lead teams."

[Alice] "Let's say we move the clock to a year from now, you have succeeded as a people manager. What does it look like? Tell me what is going on?"

[Bob] "Well, team members are excited to be in the team. They feel energised to come to work every day."

[Alice] "Energised?"

[Bob] "Yes, like when you know you have a purpose and are in the right place doing something you know you can do really well."

[Alice] "Okay, so you want to be seen as the High Energy manager."

[Bob] "Yes, like the Energizer Rabbit of the batteries."

[Alice] "Okay, should we say your goal is to be the Energizer Rabbit Manager?"

[Bob] "Sounds funny but great at the same time. Let's go with this one."

[Alice] "Okay, so let's go back to the present day. What is happening? What gets in the way of achieving that?"

[Bob] "Well, I don't know the individuals in the first place, like the type of style they are used to, or if they will like my way of working. Also, I am okay doing things at my own pace, and I am not sure how I feel about simply 'letting go.'"

[Alice] "Thanks for sharing, Bob. They sound like perfectly reasonable areas to consider when becoming a manager. What do you think you can do?"

[Bob] "I guess I could have a team session or offsite, where we spend time together as a team getting to know each other and building mutual trust. And I can share how I usually do things but also ask them for input."

[Alice] "That's a meaningful step. So what are the first actions you would take, and by when?"

[Bob] "I will send a welcome email this afternoon and book a venue for the team-building event."

[Alice] "Amazing, good luck!"

FORWARD-LOOKING AND DIRECTIVE WITH THE ATTENTION ON THE COACH

Mentorship

Although frequently treated as a separate approach to coaching, it can also be conceptualised as a type of directive coaching, where the mentor plays a role in actively shaping the solution space and defining a course of action. Mentors are usually appointed in recognition of their experience, knowledge or acumen, so they are expected to share knowledge with the less-experienced learners. During the sessions, mentors take more airtime than the learner, and dynamics focus on providing advice and guidance (from the mentor experience). Questions usually come from the learners. Advice is provided, yet there is no expectation to accept and follow it through.

These formats are common in work environments where employees are connected to mentors, who tend to be senior managers, to help their career development. Famous mentor-mentee relationships commonly mentioned in popular culture include Plato and Aristotle in ancient Greece, Martin Scorsese and Leonardo Di Caprio in Hollywood, and Pep Guardiola and Lionel Messi in Football.

The same example for Bob and Alice would look like this:

[Bob] "I have just been promoted to People Manager, and have a team of six. I haven't managed anyone before and am used to working on things on my own. I understand this is important for my career progression, so I took the opportunity without hesitation, but I now find that I don't know what to change or how to even start."

[Alice] "I understand. Well, firstly, let me tell you this is a common situation, and I can assure you most senior leaders in the organisation have been through it. I remember when I managed a team for the first time, I was terrified. So, you are not alone."

[Bob] "So how did you manage it?"

[Alice] "Well, the first thing I'll tell you is that the sensation goes away once you start getting more familiar with the team, their priorities, their styles and the general dynamics, so that will help. The other advice I would give you is to be transparent and ready to be 'vulnerable'. Be upfront and tell your team what you expect, where you can help and where you feel less secure and might need support. This would naturally create trust and help you operate in an environment where you can be yourself."

[Bob] "That's really good advice, thanks. I'll reflect on it and see how I can put it into practice."

[Alice] "My pleasure, keen to hear how you are getting along. All the best."

Sponsorship

This is arguably the most directive type of coaching. While mentors advise and non-directive coaches provide support through encouragement and listening, sponsors act and champion. They endorse a sponsee's performance and influence the sponsee's context to support achieving a particular goal. This generally manifests in creating visibility for the individual, or initiating conversations with the sponsee's manager and stakeholders, usually to help high-potential employees prepare for and advance their careers.

As for mentorship, sponsors dominate the airtime in the engagements and come with recognised experience and reputation. Some examples in popular culture include Christian Dior, one of the foremost designers of the 20th century, who nurtured the talents of Yves Saint Laurent, the designer who would become his successor;[7] Hollywood

---

7 https://www.buzzfeed.com/marycolussi/celebrity-mentor-mentee-relationships

director Steven Spielberg spring-boarded the careers of multiple others, including J.J. Abrams; or Allan Rickman and Colin Firth; Usher helped build Justin Bieber's career. This is how Bob and Alice could display it:

[Bob] "I have just been promoted to People Manager and have a team of six. I haven't managed anyone before and am used to working on things on my own. I understand this is important for my career progression, so I took the opportunity without hesitation, but I now find that I don't know what to change or how to even start."

[Alice] "Have you heard about the new manager experiential training launched last month in HQ offices? Who is your manager?"

[Bob] "Matthew, and no, I wasn't aware."

[Alice] "Well, it's supposed to be great and immersive, so you spend a full week learning tools to become great managers, and of course, networking with individuals on a similar career stage. Right after this session, I'll send a note to the organisers to book your place, and CC your manager for visibility. You can use my team's budget for the travelling and accommodation."

[Bob] "That's great. I really appreciate it."

[Alice] "After you return, you can also do some shadow sessions with some of my best managers to see them in action when addressing their teams. You shouldn't try to replicate the style but rather for inspiration on how to deliver messages and draw alignment and trust. It will be fun too. Okay?"

[Bob] "Perfect, fully appreciative of your time."

[Alice] "No problem."

FORWARD-LOOKING WITH ATTENTION ON THE RESULTS

So far, we have read about some of the most well-known coaching approaches. Coaching has proven to be an excellent aid in building confidence, self-awareness and empowering individuals to improve. However, there is a significant gap. Non-Directive Coaching types tend to be open-ended and unstructured and pose a large variability in effectiveness and speed to a solution. Directive Coaching types, on the other hand, can offer solutions, but they don't focus on gaining alignment and endorsement from the learner and can be equally varied depending on the style of the coaching professional.

We believe there is a large opportunity in the intersection of both spaces, where coaching can have the ownership, energy and resilience of a non-directive style, but with the mandate to achieve tangible results from a directive approach, we call it DELIBERATE.

With Deliberate Coaching, self-improvers would work on a coaching journey with professionals who are specially fit for the type of milestone to be achieved. This will involve a series of sessions designed with a specific purpose and anticipated outcomes upon completion. The process adheres to a standardised and scalable methodology. The coach gets direct feedback after each session, and the total compounded assessment will influence the coach's tracking record and create an incentive for further participation in these engagements. The process between learner and coach will be anonymous. Conditions and duration will be established upfront, as well as details of the process to follow. At the end of the period (usually 4-6 months), learners will be able to celebrate milestones achieved, receive achievement badges and enhance the learning profile with the insights and metrics generated in the process.

(2) THE INNERS OF DELIBERATE COACHING. THE COACHING INSTANCE. A STRONG HEART AND A HEALTHY AND CONTINUOUS PULSE.

We have studied coaching and gathered life experience. We have seen first-hand how applying coaching skills has opened multiple paths and options, produced insights, generated actions, and become the foundations for life achievements.

At the same time, although coaching principles and frameworks are practical and easy to follow, each person's journey is unique. A person often comes with expectations towards the coach or what the coaching will do for them (outcome they already have in mind). The first session will focus on setting ground rules and expectations, but also on allowing for rapport building, understanding of the background, and a real focus on the current situation, but most importantly, to find what the primary desire, the one thing that energises the person, and that will become the focus and reminder of the coaching. We call this HEART.

Once the HEART has been identified and established as the ultimate goal for the coaching sessions ahead, the focus moves into setting the PULSE. The PULSE will be everywhere, and to set it, the coach will make sure that all questions and reflections revolve and encourage the coachee to become aware, accept and embrace two key components:

- Vulnerability: Being compassionate with yourself, as we see this humble approach as the only way to step away from the "how I do things, how I act and what I know is the truth and the right way" bias and therefore able to change and listen to new perspectives and ways to achieve your desire.
- Self-love: Acceptance of yourself fully for who you are, virtues and flaws, and come to terms with the fact that your life is for you to drive and own. Treat yourself with kindness and respect, and accept that even though there will be successes and failures, you are doing the best you can, and by owning and driving the actions and decisions you feel are right, you will learn and be better each time.

The HEART and PULSE (H&P) framework is born from the belief that each individual is unique and entitled to find their own way (and pace) towards success and that each human being has the potential – with the right tools and experienced coach's guidance – to aim for and achieve a better version of themselves across any topic of interest.

H&P creates the right environment to foster a human connection and find the HEART for each individual. The emphasis shifts to igniting the PULSE at a pace tailored to the individual, encouraging them to take action and cultivate insights and outputs. All the while, we maintain a central focus on respecting our inherent human nature and capacity for growth within the coaching process.

We consider that being a great coach is a mix of science (the framework) and art (the passion and gift to be able to drive connection). The creation of our Deliberate Coaching and the HEART and PULSE method leverages best coaching practices with a clear end but doubles down on the "artistic" side of the equation.

THE SCIENTIFIC AND ARTISTIC APPROACH THAT SPARKS THE HEART FINDING AND THE PULSE SETTING

The Deliberate Coach's main goal is to build and maintain balance throughout all sessions – what we call the Coaching Instance. This will be the practice arena where the coachee and coach work consistently on each session.

Within the ecosystem, and from a principle of full engagement and commitment from both parties, the HEART would be established first. The setting of the PULSE will arise on the following interactions with the objective of not only keeping the HEART at the core – and going from strength to strength – but also creating a compounded effect of actions and results that get the coachee closer to the goal, whilst increasing self-awareness, motivation and progress on their happiness and fulfilment levels at the end of their Deliberate journey.

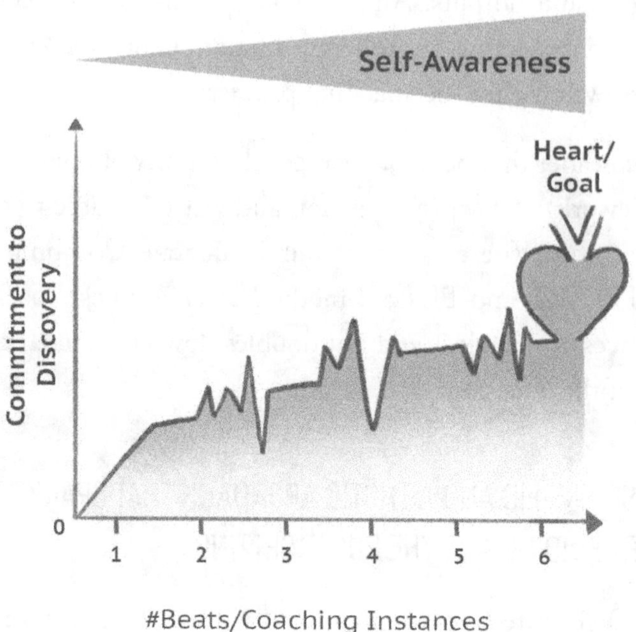

The HEART - what you desire: It is the centre of the Deliberate Coaching model. The HEART represents the goal the coachee is after. This may not be clear to the coachee at the beginning of the coaching relationship, or it could be known but diluted within other tasks. Hence, the first session of Deliberate Coaching starts with the coach supporting the coachee in unearthing the essence of the expected transformation: the authentic and energising desire that feels right.

Some examples of HEART come from real cases of courageous individuals who have embarked on this Deliberate discovery journey with us, which has made us better coaches and people whilst also being part of these coachees' dreams and goals. In no particular order:

- "This is for you."
- "I must face my fears."
- "This is my pool."
- "Expanding the network on steroids."
- "Be like a postman."
- "I feel fully motivated."
- "I want harmony."
- "Flowing"
- "The harder I work, the luckier I get."
- "Courageous Panda bear."
- "The best scrummage."

The PULSE – The pace setter. The PULSE will set the pace and give the coach a navigation route and structure to guide the coachee's journey towards the HEART. The PULSE is broken down into components allowing the coach to move the coachee through stages as necessary (and at the right pace for the coachee) on their discovery journey. Although the HEART is the ultimate goal, the PULSE is as important, given that the right pace is fundamental to get coachees to own and drive the trailblazing of their path. As long as there is a pulse, there is the possibility to improve, with driving progress and momentum.

With the H&P framework, we take the best from existing and successful coaching frameworks, but we add the experience and human layer, putting the connection to people's HEARTs at the core, and the setting of the right PULSE as the driver for success on a Deliberate journey for coachees to:

1. Embark on the pursuit of a clear and defined goal/output
2. Explore with an open, vulnerable and compassionate mindset where limitation(s) removal is encouraged
3. Create an environment that is biased for action based on "what feels right" for each individual (quantified and monitored throughout)

(3) THE LIMBS OF DELIBERATE COACHING: THE SELF-IMPROVER AND COACH EXPERIENCES

The Coachee Experience

A fundamental component of the Deliberate methodology is, of course, the learner experience, that is, anybody interested in achieving personal or professional improvements with limited time or available guidance. They can use coaching to achieve measurable results and celebrate important life milestones. They embark on a paced coaching journey with an accredited professional – who should be matched for a specific goal and learning style – following a well-proven methodology to achieve concrete life goals in six months or sooner. All this while benefiting from valuable insights and reports to support the journey.

A traditional coaching journey consists of six monthly sessions with a clear purpose and results expected at the end. The coach will get direct feedback after each session, and the total compounded assessment will influence the coach's tracking record. The process between learner and coach is anonymous, and several insights and progress cues should be available throughout. At the end of the six months, learners will be able to celebrate milestones achieved and enhance their learning profile with the insights and metrics generated in the process.

The learner would have had the opportunity to provide context about the style, aspiration and goals for the engagement, which would have prompted a number of potential coaches to be interviewed and finally decided by the coachee. Once the coach is selected, the official process of six-monthly sessions will be opened and will end with a number of insights and next steps agreed upon by both parties. The sixth and last session will be in the form of a wrap-up and will assess whether the initial goal was met, prompting an actionable summary.

This should be of high excitement for the learners because of the realisation that they will be reaching life achievements at a rate not seen before and through a truly enjoyable journey of self-discovery. Learners will acquire new tools to be the best version of themselves.

Deliberate Coaching is not only a coaching methodology; it is an enabler and connector for people who share a passion for growth and know that it is not an easy journey but one that can be better navigated together. This is why Deliberate Coaching should materially benefit from an interactive space for the community of like-minded enthusiasts (one also available for coaches) to interact and share experiences, learnings, and reflections.

The Coach Experience – User Stories and Growth Plans

Deliberate Coaching should create conditions and psychological safety where coaches and coachees can be themselves and amplify each other's chances of improving every day. This space will be a Coaching Ecosystem.

Coaches could come from all paths of life and experiences as long as they are adequately prepared (or certified), have valuable life experiences and have a willingness to learn and support others to learn alongside them. All coaches will be valued for their perspective, genuineness, but above all, the quality of their coaching preparation and abilities.

But as true believers of continuous improvement and evolution of thinking and knowledge, we dont see coaching skills in isolation nor measured against a fixed scale but as a whole and within a spectrum. To complement this, Deliberate Coaching offers an open-ended and coach-empowered certification model that encourages progression based on the following:

1. Developing coaching capabilities within the "Coaching Spectrum"

2. Building coaching experience via Deliberate Coaching journeys
3. Integrating continuous feedback and insights to improve the certification model in sprints

The accreditation ladder provides a clear path towards improvement and mastery of must-have skill sets and knowledge to become better coaches and people, as well as a defined plan with milestones to progress on the coaching journey. That said, the Deliberate Certification journey is grounded on Continuous Improvement and should be a blueprint for each coach to make it their own journey and stretch within it as they see fit and at the pace that works the best. The illustration of the ladder and a sample profile can be seen below:

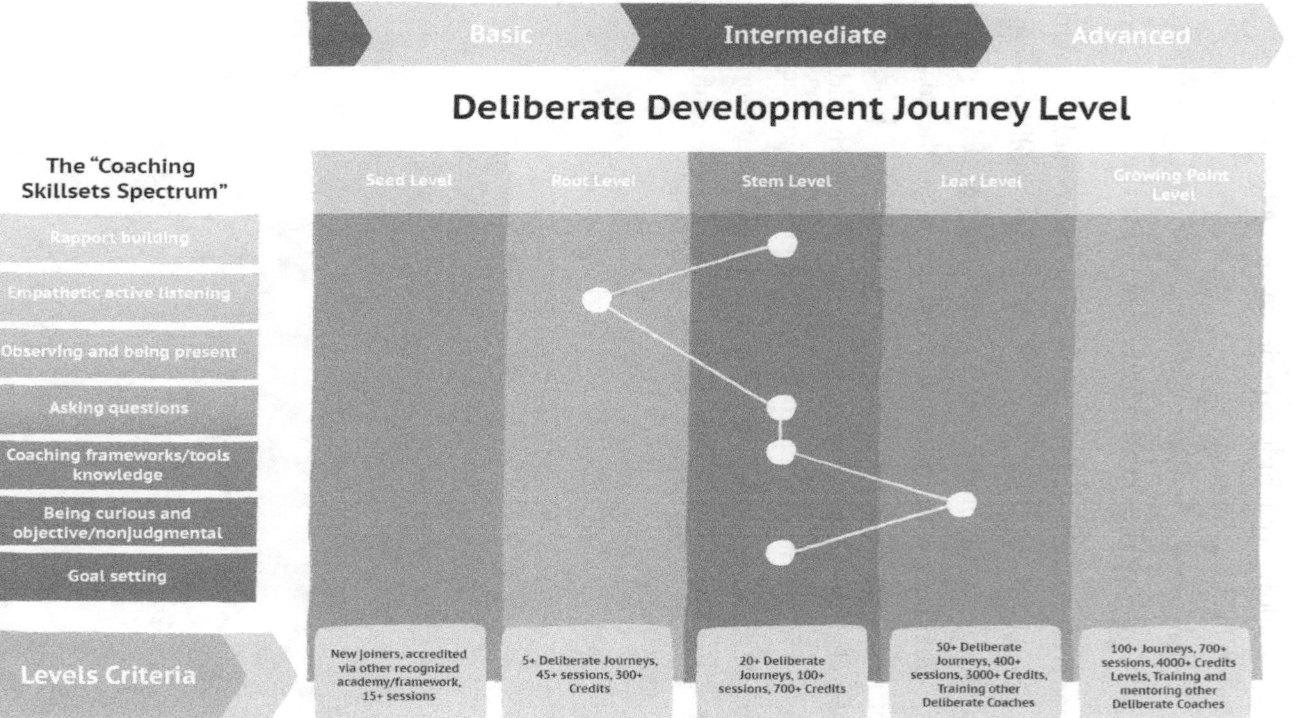
Basic
Intermediate
Advanced
Deliberate Development Journey Level
The "Coaching Skillsets Spectrum"
Rapport building
Empathetic active listening
Observing and being present
Asking questions
Coaching frameworks/tools knowledge
Being curious and objective/nonjudgmental
Goal setting
Levels Criteria
Seed Level
Root Level
Stem Level
Leaf Level
Growing Point Level
New joiners, accredited via other recognized academy/framework, 15+ sessions
5+ Deliberate Journeys, 45+ sessions, 300+ Credits
20+ Deliberate Journeys, 100+ sessions, 700+ Credits
50+ Deliberate Journeys, 400+ sessions, 3000+ Credits, Training other Deliberate Coaches
100+ Journeys, 700+ sessions, 4000+ Credits Levels, Training and mentoring other Deliberate Coaches

Based on research performed on active and aspiring coaches combined with our vision for an impactful coaching experience, Deliberate Coaching is designed to fulfil the following coaching missions.

1. Personal development (individual and universal): As a coach, I want to be able to continuously develop my listening, asking and reflecting skills to support others in the best way possible.

2. Coaching impact and personal brand development: As a coach, I want to be able to balance my energy better and focus on the facilitation of coaching sessions whilst leveraging my genuineness and personal and coaching identity.

3. Measurable and actionable insights generation: As a coach, I want access to insights from my coaching sessions to best tailor my coaching methods for my clients and provide data points and clarity on progress to my coaches.

4. Coaching performance improvement: As a coach, I want access to best practices and frameworks to enhance my coaching business performance, i.e., a view on how and when to refresh my coaching courses and approach to support my audience better.

5. Technology and systems: As a coach, I want to have a simple and pragmatic platform to manage and that provides me with the tools and intelligence to support capturing and tracking agreed actions and measuring desired HEART outcomes and goals from my coachees.

6. Consolidation of practices and community: As a coach, I want to have a community of like-minded professionals that I can reach out to, to exchange perspectives, share actionable insights from coaching results, and work alongside each other to improve the coaching service towards democratisation and accessibility.

These missions are foundations to access a flourishing market full of potential for growth and with an ever-growing segment of individuals facing a challenge that may not yet understand the untapped power to change their views with the support of a coach.

(4) THE VOICE OF DELIBERATE COACHING: AN INSIGHTS GENERATOR MACHINE

Deliberate Coaching delivers results and creates positive ripples around individuals, communities and organisations. These ripples take the form of insights that grow exponentially as the Deliberate flywheel, amplified by the Deliberate practice moves. These insights can allow HR departments and talent development organisations to adjust their hiring and development programmes when knowing:

- The most common sources of anxiety and stress in a corporate environment
- How underperforming managers and individuals rationalise and react to interventions of performance management

- What variables can be considered to enrich the environment to allow overperforming individuals to thrive
- Level of self-confidence and employee satisfaction improvement when meaningful goals are created and achieved
- How Diversity, Equity and Inclusion is perceived by employees
- The true drivers of job satisfaction, beyond promotion or salary increase
- How newly-promoted managers can best be supported to continue their progression
- How to best prepare and support professionals during meaningful transitions (region, level, manager, role).
- Styles and techniques to achieve a fruitful and sustainable work-life balance

The applicability of these principles extends well beyond the corporate realm and encompasses various life stages. This includes addressing the challenges and adjustments associated with university life, navigating through ambiguity, managing expectations, handling tight schedules, undertaking substantial projects with limited time or resources, and a myriad of other possible scenarios. The scope of possibilities is vast and diverse. We would love to hear stories of your insights. Join the community at **deliberate-coaching.com**

Chapter IV Wrap-Up:

A mental big bang

KEY LEARNING POINTS

1. Coaching adds value and augments a person's ability to achieve goals, but our proposition puts an accent on providing the rails via a "body and human" system to achieve tangible results

2. The Deliberate proposition is human-centred and its components reflect that:

   - The Brain: The body of knowledge and manifesto you are consuming right now, the manifesto that set the path towards our Deliberate north star
   - The Heart: Our methodology to support coachees on their discovery journey, one we believe creates a safe and respectful setting for coachees to be their authentic selves, feel seen, heard and valued.
   - The Arms and Legs: Represented and fuelled by learners' and coaches' experiences as they navigate their coaching journeys, providing a continuous human spark
   - The Voice: Acting as the connector to complete our system and that will feed back all insights generated

into the other components, allowing for a compound effect and virtuous cycle (positive flywheel)

3. Deliberate Coaching aims to provide a solution to people like you. A system enriched by coachees' and coaches' experiences that creates a safe ecosystem – with tools and participants – supporting each other towards raising collective and individual standards and achievement of goals/dreams in our hearts

LEARNERS' CURIOSITY REFLECTION QUESTIONS

1. What are your initial thoughts about the Deliberate Coaching proposition?

2. Is there a particular component of the system that resonated more with you or that you found more interesting?

3. Immediate response (follow your heart and don't think too much for this one) Which journey are you feeling more attracted to right now, the coaching journey or the coachee journey?

4. This evening, before falling asleep, take a minute to focus on your breathing and listen to your heart.

CHAPTER V

The Future of Deliberate Coaching

Growth is not a destination; it is a continuum. As such, Deliberate Coaching is created under an agile and never-ending, always exciting journey towards becoming better in any area of our life. This should not be a scary journey. On the contrary, it is exciting, data and success metric driven, based on experience from others in similar scenarios, that will be led by each one of you, with the proper support, to empower and develop your decision-making ability as you find the solutions that fit your circumstances.

The Deliberate ecosystem will host a team, tools and members to drive a continuous improvement mindset that allows for the achievement of all participants' individual success, leveraging everyone's insights towards collective deliberate achievements.

Every person, regardless of socio-economic background, education level, professional area of speciality, life experience, religious beliefs or lack thereof, is living their life and doing the best to live with integrity and resilience despite multiple challenges and feelings.

In the end, we are all quintessentially human, with virtues and flaws, and plough through our days with something – coming from our hearts – that gives us the strength to make each day work. As we put ourselves out there, we want to be seen, heard, and understood. This isn't just fair—it's our right. It validates us, gives us dignity, and adds meaning to our lives as we do our best.

Many of us know this at some level but do not necessarily exploit this awareness to a point where we can take a step back to reflect on what we really want to achieve, and how we could evolve via exploring with deliberate support from others.

We want to spark the fire of a Deliberate Coaching mindset within each individual, to hand you the match to light it.

We believe in believe in humans' potential to:

1. Improve and evolve their thinking and acting whilst also supporting others to find new perspectives
2. Be vulnerable to accept that we are all a work in progress, and be compassionate to accept that our "truth and reality" today are not fixed
3. Leverage technology as an accelerator for evolution

4. Understand that awareness is key to staying open to chance and that there is a path towards not being a "robot" and permanently stuck to the same beliefs

There isn't a definitive blueprint for the next manifestation of humanity, but in the collective tapestry of individuals existing today, there are those who pause to question our cherished and seemingly secure truths, opting for the uncertainty that accompanies the pursuit of a better, more evolved self. However, the real future of the Deliberate world is not based on individual achievements but on a collective conscious effort to leverage the success factors that were right for the Deliberate coachees and coaches in the spaces covered, e.g. parenting, time management, decision making, conflict management and child trauma.

Moreover, the future transcends mere coaching. We aspire to propel behavioural change, seeking a universal platform that amalgamates the finest facets of human thinking. Here, mentoring, therapy, psychology, coaching, and established methodologies converge, collaborating seamlessly towards a singular and paramount objective – the pursuit of individual wisdom and perpetual learning for the betterment of a consciously aware society. Deliberate Coaching is a one-to-stop shop where a culture of growth and achievement resides, fuelled by a rich mix of business, education, and life experiences from everyone who is part of the collective/community, and we can only but expand and pass on the torch with our example and model to continue igniting the Deliberate learning spark to at least one more person.

Our future relies on your eagerness to join this wave of awakening, and we believe in your potential to grow and learn as you support the growth of those walking this Deliberate journey alongside you.

Chapter V Wrap-Up:

All together now

KEY LEARNING POINTS

1. Personal growth and development across any area of our lives is a continuum, and coaching gives the springboard to achieve meaningful results over a period of time

2. The Deliberate proposition and positive flywheel provides a shared space to navigate their own journeys towards growth, leveraging coaching tools, expertise and a community of coaches and coachees open and willing to support each other to raise everyone's standards

3. The future of Deliberate Coaching is still to be written yet will be defined by everyone involved in it. The goal is to grow and include as many people as possible and use the insights from their journeys to drive the evolution of the Deliberate principles.

CHAPTER VI

Case Study
Striving for Change - A "Motivated" Journey

Andrew is an experienced manager of a global corporation who has an Information Systems background and currently acts as an IT Manager. He approached his coach – Quijote – via LinkedIn. Andrew did not have a clear goal in mind beyond the idea that he needed a change; at a very high level he felt compelled towards career progression and potentially pivoting from his technical oriented role to a more business focused one.

It all started with a quick 15-minute chat, and when Quijote saw Andrew's humble attitude, proactivity, and curiosity, he felt they were both ready to begin a proper coaching journey; therefore, he invited him to have a first connect call to explore his current expectations and goals.

THE FIRST BEAT - WHAT IS GOING ON?

[Quijote]: "Hi Andrew, how are you?"

[Andrew]: "I am good, thank you. I am super excited about this meeting. How are you?"

[Quijote]: "I am very happy to see you after all these years and keen to hear what you are doing these days. So tell me, what is going on?"

[Andrew]: "Well, not really sure where to start, to be honest. I have been working for this company for five years now and feel a bit stuck in my current role."

[Quijote]: "Stuck, you say..."

[Andrew]: "Yes, I have been an IT Manager since I joined, and I feel ready to take a new role, one that allows me to lead a team."

[Quijote]: "It sounds like you want to push your boundaries and lead others. Please tell me how you feel when you lead others."

[Andrew]: (Pauses for a few seconds) "I feel motivated!" His tone is different from before, one that reflects impetus and energy.

[Quijote]: "Can you repeat that and listen to yourself as you say it?"

[Andrew]: "I feel motivated!"

[Quijote]: "Wow, what a boost of energy, Andrew! You do sound motivated. Please continue. Where do you see yourself when you feel motivated?"

[Andrew]: "I see myself with a large team, guiding and leading them. Using my experience as an IT manager to help them grow in their careers, and setting direction on where we need to go to achieve our goals.

[Quijote]: "Okay, it sounds like you have a clear goal here: to expand your role to become a team leader and help them grow under your direction?"

[Andrew]: (Pauses for a few seconds) "Yes, absolutely, Quijote."

[Quijote]: "Great, let me tell you something. I have found it beneficial to assign phrases or words to a goal as a way for coachees to remind themselves of what they're striving for. It is only normal to have moments where we might lack the disposition to push and do what it takes to achieve our goals... What should we call or refer to when thinking about this one?"

[Andrew]: "Interesting, I don't know, but I felt motivated when I thought about it earlier... That's it, MOTIVATED! That is going to be the word for this goal."

[Quijote]: "Excellent, Andrew! So, we have the 'motivated' goal now. What else is happening with you right now? Are there other areas you would like to change in your life?"

[Andrew]: There is something, actually. Not sure if it's directly related but it is about spending more quality time and being more present with my family."

[Quijote]: "Please elaborate, Andrew..."

[Andrew]: "I have two small children. They are eight and four years old. My wife and I do our best every day to be there for them but we both work, so it is challenging most of the time. I take the little one to nursery in the mornings, but on most occasions, we are rushing… (then he pauses for a bit and continues) And I just feel that I am not really there, like I am but just not fully present."

[Quijote]: "Okay, so it sounds like you would like to work out a different dynamic for your morning drop-offs so that you can be more present and enjoy the experience beyond just doing it rushed. Is that fair?"

[Andrew]: "That's it! I need to change my morning routine. I see my personal and professional life as two sides of the same coin. If I can make this change in addition to being more present and enjoying the moment with my little one in the morning, I will be in a better position to organise my mind and be ready for work."

[Quijote]: "Interesting, Andrew. How would you like to call this goal?"

[Andrew]: "Energised Present Mornings!"

[Quijote]: "This sounds great, Andrew. I am conscious of time. Is there any other goal?"

[Andrew]: "I don't think so, not for now, at least."

[Quijote]: "Okay, good. Which one would you like to start with first?"

[Andrew]: "Energised Present Mornings, I see this one more precisely."

[Quijote]: "What is clear about this one? Do you have any actions already in mind then?"

[Andrew]: "As a matter of fact, I do. I am going to wake up earlier in the mornings to bring the schedule forward by 45 minutes. This way, I think we can both benefit from a calmer experience."

[Quijote]: "Okay, Andrew, does this require effort only from you? What do you think is the key for you to accomplish this?"

[Andrew]: "Actually, it's a very good question. No, I need him engaged too. Good point. The key is for us both to be consistent, resilient and willing to make it happen and stick with it. I will make it fun. I will transform this into a 'fun challenge' for him."

[Quijote]: "Brilliant! It sounds like you have an action to think about – how to create a fun challenge for you and your little one. When will you do this?"

[Andrew]: "By our connect next week, I will define a fun challenge for the school drop-offs in the mornings."

[Quijote]: "I look forward to speaking to you then, Andrew, and to listening to your energised Present Moment Fun Challenge!"

THE SECOND BEAT – ENERGISED PRESENT MORNING FUN CHALLENGE

[Quijote]: "Hello, Andrew. How was your week?"

[Andrew]: "It was tricky but good. I thought about my situation at work a bit more, and some ideas came to mind. I felt a bit nervous and worried when doing so, but in order to move away from the anxiety of those thoughts, I went into the fun challenge for the drop-offs and would like us to start there today."

[Quijote]: "Let us hear the fun challenge first. Then, we definitely want to start on the right foot."

[Andrew]: "Well, my little one likes this cartoon named Inspector Gadget a lot. You may remember it as it has been out there for decades. So, I made him think our journey to school was a quest for clues as we walked there. Given that there were quite a few trees and gardens on the way, I made us bring a magnifying glass with us the other morning, and we stopped occasionally to check on leaves or rocks. We obviously left home earlier than usual, and I think that inviting him to the quest the previous night and giving him the magnifying glass helped us both wake up earlier and get ready sooner. That and the fact that I set the alarm an hour before, but I had done that in the past and snoozed it until there was no time, so..."

[Quijote]: "So what?"

[Andrew]: "So I think I kind of tricked myself without realising."

[Quijote]: "Interesting, Andrew. Tell me more about how you think you tricked yourself."

[Andrew]: "Well, I had put the alarm on earlier before but that didn't work. This time, I was looking forward to getting ready. I wanted to be present and feel it with him as we went to school together."

[Quijote]: "It sounds like you had fun yourself."

[Andrew]: "I did have a lot of fun, not just on the day but also planning it."

[Quijote]: "Great to hear. So, will you continue doing it now that you know it is possible?"

[Andrew]: "Absolutely, I only did it on Friday and yesterday (Monday) but I am already thinking of ideas on how to create other activities to keep us both energised. For now, I do know that I loved listening to him and playing along as we walked and 'explored'."

[Quijote]: "Exploring together seems like something to keep you happy and energised. I can definitely feel it in your voice right now. This is great progress, and I'm really pleased for you."

[Andrew]: Thank you, Quijote. I feel very, very good about this indeed."

[Quijote]: "Andrew, I don't want to rain on your parade but you also said you felt very worried and anxious about the work goal. In a way, it worked to get you to make progress somewhere else, but I think it's probably good to at least touch on it today, even if briefly, and we continue into the next session if you are okay with it."

[Andrew]: "Yes, that's fine. I want to at least try to articulate it but I am unsure if I can."

[Quijote]: "Try me, and we can drop it at any point if you don't feel like using our remaining time on it today."

[Andrew]: "I definitely want to change, I do. It has been too long doing this role, and I want to grow as I help a team of people grow with me. But I feel stuck. My boss is not listening to me when I tell him I want to do more and support him in planning more strategic activities. The more I try to explain this to him, the more he shuts me down, and I feel worried now because it looks like he is getting annoyed with me and avoiding the conversation."

[Quijote]: "You say he shuts you down. How do you know he is shutting you down?"

[Andrew]: "Last time when I brought this to him over TEAMS in preparation for our one-to-one weekly meeting, he did not even acknowledge the message and then ended up pushing out the one-to-one session by a week. When we finally connected, he did not say anything about the last-minute change or my TEAMS message of growth opportunities. It had to be me bringing this up again, and after listening to me, he did not give me any solutions."

[Quijote]: "Does he have to give you the solution?"

[Andrew]: (Long pause) "Well, no, I mean, but he did not even acknowledge the changes in the session."

[Quijote]: "I get it. It is frustrating not to feel heard."

[Andrew]: "Exactly, he is not even listening. How can he find me a solution?"

[Quijote]: "Interesting, Andrew. Can I share a perspective with you?"

[Andrew]: "Yes, sure, please do."

[Quijote]: "It is completely understandable to feel frustrated when not able to make one's point understood by someone else, but sometimes when the other person can't understand our point, it is because we have not been able to articulate how important it is to us. Also, it may be that we could be expecting the person to take an action or solve the problem, when in reality, the action may be for you to find alternatives to explore rather than seeking solutions from someone else."

[Andrew]: (Long silence) "I think I understand. Let me take this away."

[Quijote]: "Of course, I will leave you with this as I believe in you and have seen during these couple of sessions that you can articulate what you want and need from others to get that. Let us connect this week, but please think about what you wish for this goal in one sentence, and how your boss can help/support you to achieve it."

[Andrew]: "Thanks, Quijote, I will do it."

THE THIRD BEAT – FINDING AND VISUALISING THE MOTIVATED BELIEF AND "THE ASK"

[Andrew]: "Hi Quijote, before we start, I wanted to thank you for our last session. It left me thinking about many things, and I have reflected a lot since then."

[Quijote]: "This is music to my ears, Andrew. These are the best sessions, in my opinion, and to be honest with you, I felt something special, which I was hoping would open up some new ideas."

[Andrew]: "It absolutely did, and I will go straight into it. I think I was too much in my own head, and I have not given myself the opportunity to clearly articulate the request to my boss because I felt it would put me at a disadvantage."

[Quijote]: "Can you please elaborate a bit more, Andrew?"

[Andrew]: "Well, I have no proven experience in a leadership position. I have plenty of experience as a manager but never had direct reports, so there are blind spots when it comes to managing people, and I realised I did not want to say this to him."

[Quijote]: "Thank you for sharing this, Andrew. I fully understand that being vulnerable does not come naturally to many people, and could be perceived as a weakness. Although, I think vulnerability is the first step to great things, so I appreciate you doing it now. So, you are now aware of this blind spot around managing others, this is an improvement for self-awareness. How does this help articulate the ask to your boss?"

[Andrew]: "Good question. First, let me tell you that my goal and what I want are still unchanged. The more I reflected, the more I felt motivated to make this change happen. So MOTIVATED is how I feel and want to be in my life and new role."

[Quijote]: "Go on. I'm completely motivated here too!"

[Andrew]: "When I came to him for support, I realised that I was somewhat waiting for him to solve this for me and tell me how and where to go to find this role. When in reality, it has to come from me. No one but me can really know where to go next."

[Quijote]: "What a statement, Andrew. I feel there is more."

[Andrew]: "There is. I know that when I started working after I finished university, I lacked experience in my current role, but somehow, I managed to build up my skills to a point where I was becoming more confident by the day. The thing is… I don't feel I can do it again."

[Quijote]: "Okay, your experience after university is quite a good example. Can you give me a more recent one where you also built up your skills from nothing?"

[Andrew]: "Erghh…" (Long pause) "A few years ago, I wanted to start running properly, as in marathon level."

[Quijote]: "Excellent, I am assuming you did it. What pulled you?"

[Andrew]: "Sure I did. I ran the Berlin Marathon. It took a full year of preparation, a lot of early mornings, healthy eating and mental strength, especially for the rainy days."

[Quijote]: "Are you open to doing a visualisation exercise, Andrew? I think there is something here for you."

[Andrew]: "Let's do it. What do I need to do?"

[Quijote]: "Switch off your camera, and I will do the same, then close your eyes and follow my lead."

---- VISUALISATION EXERCISE FACILITATED BY QUIJOTE ----

[Quijote]: "How do you feel now, Andrew? Any thoughts before we wrap up for today?"

[Andrew]: "Wow, I feel I am still running. I can feel the rush and the energy in my body as if I just ran 10k and am now relaxing and stretching with full knowledge that I can definitely do this. I will do it because it is in my hands, and no obstacle can stop me."

[Quijote]: "Motivated despite any obstacles for sure. I look forward to our next session, Andrew."

THE FOURTH BEAT – REAPING THE MOTIVATED BENEFITS, ANGLING FOR THE NEW ROLE TRANSFER

For context, it is worth noting that Quijote created a WhatsApp group called "Motivated 2023" and shared some reflection questions with Andrew to work on in addition to the usual session summary email.

[Andrew]: "Hi Quijote, thanks for the questions. I have reflected so much since we last connected."

[Quijote]: "Hi Andrew, I am thrilled for you and how motivated you seem to be now that you have found insights."

[Andrew]: "Well, yes, it has been tough to find the time and do the work, but I have done quite a few things at work. The situation with my boss still feels a bit frosty. However, I sat with him on our one-to-one this past week and explained that I understood and respected his views about my current role but that I felt motivated and ready to take on a new challenge within the team, and would appreciate his support for me to explore moves within the company."

[Quijote]: "Andrew, this is a great step. You have not only taken the reigns here but also faced head-on what I know was a difficult conversation in a very mature way. Was he receptive?"

[Andrew]: "Did I? I guess I did, yes. I never thought I could a few months ago, but yes, I did but it was super stressful, to be honest. For the first time in a long time, he paid attention to what I was saying, and I finally felt heard. However, I was anxious and felt threatened on occasions but I breathed and remembered the calm I felt after a long run, and that helped me stay centred. Anyway, he was honest with me and told me he did not want me to leave and join another team but that he understood my position and that if I already had an area or team in mind, to please let him know."

[Quijote]: "I am hearing that you took the time to articulate your ask, faced a conversation that was avoided for quite some time and managed to get your point across, Andrew."

[Andrew]: (Long pause) "Because I am motivated and ready to take the initiative whatever the consequences."

[Quijote]: "It certainly looks like that from where I am standing. Look at the results you are achieving! Did you agree on the next steps?"

[Andrew]: "Yes, we did. I am going to reach out to the UK Centre of Excellence (CoE) team with whom I have had a couple of conversations in the past and who hinted to me on the last one that he would be open to discussing my joining his team if that was something of interest to me. I agreed with my boss that I would think about a transition plan for someone taking on my role."

[Quijote]: "Excellent, Andrew. Is there anything else?"

[Andrew]: "I don't think so, no."

[Quijote]: "Okay, then let us wrap up for today. Allow me to congratulate you on your progress. You have come a long way, and I feel thankful to witness these results."

[Andrew]: "Thank you. It is definitely a shared journey, and I appreciate all the support and trust, Quijote."

[Quijote]: "My pleasure Andrew. Speak soon."

THE FIFTH BEAT – TACKLING OTHER CURVE BALLS, EXTRAPOLATING PROFESSIONAL SKILLS TO PERSONAL CHALLENGES – CHANGING BEHAVIOURS

[Quijote]: "Hello Andrew. How are you? What would you like us to focus our time on today?"

[Andrew]: "Hi, I am good, thank you. Although I'm a bit down for some reason. I have progressed with my conversation with the CoE team. It was a good one. I feel very positive about this one and should hear from them in a few weeks' time. I have also done a draft transition plan document that I have shared with my boss, and I started to participate more and be more vocal in meetings, which is another thing I wanted to start doing."

[Quijote]: "This is what I call a motivation and momentum combo right there. Glad to hear of this newfound clarity. Well done. But you said that you feel a bit down too. Do you want to tell me more about that?"

[Andrew]: "Yes, actually, I think I would like to use today's session for this."

[Quijote]: "Let us do that then."

[Andrew]: "As I said, I'm not sure where to start. I don't know why I feel this drained and tired in the evenings. I think work changes and new conversations are a part of it, but I feel motivated by these changes. I see light at the end of the tunnel finally, so it is not that."

[Quijote]: "What else has been happening outside work? How is the family?"

[Andrew]: "All is well at home. The school drop-off dynamic is settled now, and I have managed to find time for my eldest in the evening as well, so it is balanced. Even my wife mentioned the other day that she is pleasantly surprised with my new approach."

[Quijote]: "This sounds all very positive. Anything else?"

[Andrew]: "Yes, I spoke to my dad the other day over the phone. The usual call to check in on him. However, we landed on a topic where we have disagreed for some time now. I have been thinking about it. Perhaps that's the cause."

[Quijote]: "Okay, what did you speak about?"

[Andrew]: "It is about his retirement. He has worked all his life, and I told him he should retire and that I would be happy to support him financially or otherwise, but he does not want to."

[Quijote]: "I would suggest we do an exercise to explore this conversation and prepare you for the real one when/if you are ready to have it."

[Andrew]: "I'm definitely up for this. What do I do?"

--- COACHING A THIRD ENTITY EXERCISE FACILITATED BY QUIJOTE -----

[Quijote]: "How do you feel now?"

[Andrew]: "That was intense but actually I feel very relieved now."

[Quijote]: "I completely understand, Andrew, but you have actually got an idea of how this conversation could go? I think it would be great if you take time to let all those insights sink in."

[Andrew]: "Thank you, Quijote. I will certainly do that. See you at our next session."

THE SIXTH BEAT – CELEBRATING THE TRANSITION, A PROFESSIONAL AND PERSONAL CHANGE

[Andrew]: "Morning, Quijote. As mentioned over the WhatsApp group, I found the opportunity to talk with my dad, and it was a great conversation. By the end, I felt we had connected at a deeper level and now understand and accept each other's perspectives.

[Quijote]: "This is lovely to hear, Andrew. As it is our last session, it will be good to hear what you have learned and achieved over this period."

[Andrew]: "It's incredible how fast it has all gone. To be honest, I did not think I would be able to do so much."

[Quijote]: "And imagine how much more you are capable of doing with this new motivated self you have found within you!"

[Andrew]: "I can certainly say I have found a new gear; I am more confident and motivated to keep making things happen for me. I accept my limitations, but do not feel blocked by them; I am actually empowered and motivated to see beyond them and explore new unchartered territories. By the way, my conversations with my boss about a change in the team and my role is pretty much on track. Also, at a personal level, I see happiness in my family, and I feel fulfilled and thankful."

[Quijote]: "Andrew, these are big achievements you are calling out here, and I can tell from your energy that they come from your heart. Well done for allowing yourself to be vulnerable, coming to the sessions, but also doing the work and taking action. This is all on you."

[Andrew]: "I was able to find the path, and now I have tools and a blueprint thanks to our work together."

[Quijote]: "I may have pushed you gently, yes but you permitted me to do so. However, thanks for the acknowledgement. I am here whenever you need me in the future. But talking about the future, what is the plan with all this motivation and the achievements you have acquired? I am curious."

[Andrew]: "Mmmhhh… that is a really good question, Quijote! You never stop, do you?"

[Quijote]: "Sorry, guilty as charged, but you know me by now."

[Andrew]: "Well, at the top of my head, I will be planning my new role in the first 90 days in the new team as I expect this to materialise within the next month or so. I will then make sure I keep myself available to my family, and am present for them making every moment a special one."

[Quijote]: "This definitely resonates with me. Thanks for sharing, Andrew. I can tell you from my side that accompanying you on this journey has been an absolute privilege, and that I wish you the very best in the future. Please don't forget that if ever in doubt, just listen to your heart, and remember that lovely story you told me about running!"

[Andrew]: "Thanks so much, Quijote. Let us definitely stay in touch, and I really appreciate your support over this period."

[Quijote]: "You are welcome, and don't be a stranger. Always stay motivated! Bye."

PART 2

HAY LITTLE PIGGY DESIGNS THE CHELSEA STADIUM

A DELIBERATE COACHING STORY

CHARACTER PORTRAITS

INTRODUCING THE CAST THAT WILL TAKE YOU ON A
DELIBERATE JOURNEY IN THE COMING PAGES

CHAPTER 1

10 Human-Equivalent Years after Liberation Day

I

Never again in the life of Edgard-the-Pig would a Roasted Cauliflower taste as good as the one from that afternoon. It might have been the hunger since he had been outside foraging for food for most of the day, or the warmth of the fireplace (yes, the famous one), knowing how cold and windy it was outside, or maybe the tiredness from playing Piggy Tail with his little nephews Romy and Jonny Piglets. Probably, it was simply the special occasion of the last family supper before the big trip. The truth of the matter is that Edgard-the-Pig and the family feasted and celebrated that afternoon like they hadn't in a long time.

"Tell us again the story of the Chicken-Wolf, Uncle Edgard. I like your version better than Dad's," said Romy-the-Piglet.

"You mean the Marinated Roasted Wolf?" said Jonny-the-Piglet, giggling.

"No, no, no, please," said Bruce-the-Pig, who was in the back fetching some logs, with his characteristic deep voice. "I already told the story four times this week. It feels like work. Besides, your Uncle Edgard always blushes red when we tell it. At least he doesn't clean the windows anymore. He used to do it as a teenager as a symbol of protest. Can you believe it?"

"Because you were obsessed with your mud and could not stop bothering him," said William-the-Pig, who had to stop rubbing his belly momentarily to catch his breath.

"Hey, it's not my fault that the town started calling him Sticky Wind," replied Bruce-the-Pig.

"Are you going to tell the story or not, then?" chanted Jonny and Romy piglets almost in unison.

"Well, okay. I'm sure after tomorrow I won't be stopped in the street for an autograph or an olfaction. Let this be the last time in a while," added Edgard-the-Pig.

By then, Romy and Jonny piglets had found their places in their scruffy bin bags in the living room while Bruce and William grabbed a cup of Scottish Sludge and joined them by the fireplace, ready to hear the story of the Three Little Piggies for the hundredth time.

||

"I am the Big Bad Wolf. If you don't let me come in, I'LL HUFF AND I'LL PUFF AND I'LL BLOW YOUR HOUSE IN!" Then Uncle Edgard-the-Pig stood on the high stool and put on the black rubbery bag. It was a standard grocery bag but the piglets had carved holes converting it into a mask. He inhaled as much air as he could – which wasn't much because pigs have very tiny lungs – and then made the loudest noise ever which in reality sounded like a giant burp with crumbs thrown away into the air.

"Hahahaha, oink oink," clapped the piglets after they passed the scare of the moment into cheeky laughter.

"What I don't understand, Uncle Edgard, is why you built your house from stalks? Even we little piglets don't use it to pretend fight with swords because it breaks very easily," said Jonny Piglet.

"Because he is Lazy!" grunted William-the-Pig with laughter. "He just wanted to play and sing all day, so when he found that man carrying a bundle of straw, he saw the easy way out and the cheapest too."

"What a foolish thing to do!" added Bruce-the-Pig. "Everyone in the village knew the Wolf was on the prowl. Actually, Mayor Pig had even raised taxes to be able to pay for the Groundhog Police to try to keep him away from the town. And here comes Clever Edgard and builds his house with sticks and hay. Probably even a turtle would have blown it away if she had got there faster than the Wolf."

Everybody laughs at the silly joke.

"Okay, okay, okay! I deserve it," said Edgard-the-Pig. "Let's say I acted as the decoy so you can see what the Wolf was capable of."

"In any case," said Edgard-the-Pig, directing the conversation to Jonny and Romy piglets, "it was a long time ago, and I was not much older than what you are now. Although people in the village called us the Three Little Pigs, my brothers, William and Bruce Pigs, were not only older and bigger, but they were more responsible and hard-working. You see, our mother asked us to find a place and build our dream homes, and each made our own choices and learned our own lessons. If it wasn't for Bruce-the-Pig and his vision to build a house of Bricks with this nice and big Fireplace, we would probably have ended in the Christmas celebration of the Wolf Family."

"PIG BRUCE CAME TO THE RESCUE!" shouted Jonny and Romy piglets.

"Sir Pig Bruce, dear Piglets, Sir Pig Bruce…" grunted Bruce-the-Pig from the corner of the room while contemplating the large photograph in the centre of the wall.

"What happened then, Uncle Edgard?" asked the piglets.

"Well, you know the story of the Wolf and what happened in the Village after… I am not going to inflate Sir Pig Bruce's ego any more. I will tell you though, that this was a giant lesson for me, and that incident helped me make important decisions for my life," reflected Edgard-the-Pig.

"Like to become an *aqueduct*? We want to know why you became that," asked Romy Piglet.

"ARCHITECT!" replied Edgard-the-Pig, smiling. "And that reminds me that I need to check my train for the big trip tomorrow."

The Three Little Pigs' Tale: Lessons, Laughter, and the Big Bad Wolf

Liberation Day is how it became engraved in the history books – the day in which the Big Bad Wolf unsuccessfully tried to blow the house that Bruce-the-Pig built. He used the latest materials found in the Forrest Depot but mainly sturdy columns and solid old-school bricks. Not only was it embarrassing for the Wolf since the entire village was watching from their windows and peepholes, but it got worse when the Wolf and his wounded pride tried to enter through the fireplace, only to find a clever trap waiting for him at the bottom. He could barely escape, and when he did, his tail and bright trousers were on fire, so he had no other choice but to run, never to be seen again. Legend goes that he was not even allowed to return to his pack and had to wander the forest for years until he found a job at a local petrol station, which humans use to put fuel inside their noisy machines.

The story of the Three Little Pigs became the story of the Village, and as expected, Bruce-the-Pig was the hero and Edgard-the-Pig the what-not-to-do example. When the Forest Council finally declared the village Wolf-Free Territory, the frenzy started, and the story became legendary. The town was inundated by TV and radio stations, all wanting to take a peek, interview the hero, and take a shot in front of the famous house, which was later declared a World Pig Heritage Site, ensuring its preservation and protection for future generations. It even got a blue plaque to commemorate the Liberation.

Bruce-the-Pig always had an outgoing and interesting personality, so this event and the spotlight suited him perfectly. He published a book with the story of the house, which became the largest grossing book written by a Pig in history, even surpassing medieval behemoth Don PigXote, the reference for Pig literature. He sold the rights for a captivating TV Series in the form of a thriller, *Piggy Heist: Hunting the Hunter*, which got more views than the luminary *Peppa Pig* series at its best moment. He used this popularity to influence the Forest Society, fought for Pigs' rights, and was knighted by the Queen Pig in a widely televised ceremony. He was even named *TIME Animal of the Year* for his notoriety as a Quadruped Protector.

Despite the haloed fame and recognition that Bruce-the-Pig brought to the family, this was far from being an exciting and nurturing environment for Edgard-the-Pig to come of age. Rather introverted, thoughtful and with a general lack of self-confidence, Edgard-the-Pig was constantly overshadowed by the personality and charisma that his brothers imposed, which was augmented by the constant recreation of the event of that infamous afternoon, where the fates of the Wolf and Edgards' positivity would end up severely wounded for the years to come. On the positive side, the pig brothers were considered part of the village patrimony, so they got many sources of financial support, from the taxpig, donations and sponsorships, which at least removed the burden of any financial concerns for education and well-being.

Our shadow hero, Edgard-the-Pig, went to high school, one different from his brothers, that focused on liberal arts and the "realisation of the Pig as an individual" or so he said. But in reality, it was well known that he wanted to avoid the big crowds and be in a place as far as possible from the radius of his brothers.

Unlike many of his classmates, young Edgard-the-Pig was keen on arts and maths because he found them complementary to each other. His drawings were full of symmetries, patterns and organised colourful shapes. His tail-writing was neat, and his pig-trotter-calligraphy was accurate and full of rhythm. Among all, he was full of imagination; one just had to pick any notebook and would very likely find a seemingly random yet artistic shape that he would draw during his daydreaming moments, which were far too many.

Edgard-the-Pig also sought to learn about the real world around him – the materials, sounds, textures, and the simple structures that gave colour to this world. Suddenly, the curvature of the apple he loved so much, the spikiness and firmness of the branches, the moist feel of the meadow, and many other features of his surroundings started having a special meaning. He didn't know what all that meant then, and it would take some time until this happened. He knew he should probably be studying his timetables or reading more highbrow Pig literature, but somehow spending this time in nature and letting the mind wander felt very comforting.

Edgard-the-Pig struggled to grasp and memorise facts and events and find inspiration or exciting stories to cling to for all the other subjects required deep concentration.

With lots of effort and persistent curiosity, Edgard-the-Pig sailed through those formative years, always trying to have fun but not so much to attract the attention of the crowd. He wanted to move past the Little Piggy whose house was blown first, and embrace normality. After a while, even without Edgard-the-Pig actively doing anything about it, it just happened. The generation changed, and these new student piggies became drawn into the lure of modernity, victims of the attention economy that kept them attached to swine social media and other virtual gadgets.

IV

Along came the time for Edgard-the-Pig to take the *Pig College Acceptance Test*. This was one of the most defining moments in any pig's life since it would determine the subject and institute of study and, thus, the profession to which the swine would proudly adhere for the rest of his life – if he passed successfully, of course. In Edgard's mind, not passing the test would be a reason for shame, almost as big as not taking the test at all, and Edgard-the-Pig was not willing to bring another chapter of failure to his life. For many, it was the moment of earning the respect of the Village, the piglet becoming the Hog.

During two long hours, which for pigs' lives was a monumental amount of time – the human equivalent would be 20 times more – farrow applicants would undertake several activities in front of a "mud panel" consisting of four or five prominent hogs with proven knowledge across all kinds of disciplines and professions, who at the end would go to the corral (a specially designed deliberation space) and allocate marks and professions (or lack of) to all applicants. This was a millenary ritual that remains as relevant as ever for the pigs of the world.

His middle brother William-the-Pig, the same one who built the house with wood, took the test two years ago for medical school and got a Carrot[++], which in the Pig Educational system would equate to an A+ in the human system – or so it is believed since no humans have been allowed to read for a degree in the Pig College yet. Probably because no one has learned how to grunt and communicate with pigs. In any case, William-the-Pig not only was a great student but also became a great physician, which was very rare among the pig population. Some think this is due to the difficulty of handling medical tools with only two fingers, but not William. He managed to train himself to manipulate even lasers and high-precision gadgets, and started quite a notable medical practice in the Village, attracting hundreds of pigs from other towns to be treated by Dr William Pig.

This might have been why the Liberation story didn't seem to take a toll on William's personality. In his very own terms, William managed to redeem himself by finding a route to bring prestige and recognition to the Village by adding a personal narrative, completely disassociated from the Three Little Pigs and his house of wood. I wonder if Edgard has ever asked William about his drive to achieve this, but it was certainly a source of admiration for Edgard, especially at this defining juncture.

There it was, Edgard-the-Pig, following the steps of a Lord and a Doctor, about to hear his future from Honorary Dean Porkett Hog, an eminent scientist and statesman, famous for the invention of the Vegetarian Bacon, which is believed to have saved more than 25% of the existing world population and their future generations. Edgard still recalls Porkett's exact words:

"Student 301179, Edgard Bartolomeu Pig, your mark is Cabbages[++] and will be reading for: ARCHITECTURE…. We wish you a successful future. The Pig Society counts on you."

V

"I still cannot pronounce that word, Uncle Edgard: A.R.C.H.I.T.E.C.T.U.R.E. Why is that difficult? And how scary Dean Porkett sounded," said Jonny Piglet.

"It should be called TUPSI, instead. It's catchy and easy to remember," giggled Romy Piglet.

"You should have seen Edgard's face when he found out… like he had seen a ghost in the farm. His snout turned blue all of a sudden. Almost ready to be a muppet next to Miss Piggy Oink," added Bruce.

The room erupts in laughter.

"Of course, I was terrified. The Little Piggy who couldn't build a sturdy house for himself is now going to build houses, or bridges or tunnels, or schools, or hospitals for OTHER pigple?"

Edgard-the-Pig just wanted to disappear in a quicksand of mud right there.

"Edgard! You will scare the piglets. What matters is that you overcame your fear, and here we are celebrating. Why don't you tell them that part of the story? We need brave and self-confident piglets in this family." William-the-Pig pointed out.

"Cheers to that," saluted Bruce-the-Pig from the back of the room.

"You are right," said Edgard-the-Pig. He took a sip of mugffee, a deep breath and then resumed, "University is a very interesting and special place. There is something for everyone, so many activities, things going on and rooms, oh piglord, so many rooms. One for studying, a different one for every subject, one for relaxing, a gym, outdoor courts, lecture rooms… I lost track. I found it overwhelming and difficult during the first few terms. Don't get me wrong, I was trying but it was hard to keep up with everything that was going on. I thought it was normal initially but started having suspicions when the head of the department called me to her office to assign me a 'coach', since this could help me get on track and 'in control' as she put it," explained Edgard-the-Pig.

"Like the Trotterball coaches that we see on Sundays shouting at the players and taking them out of the pitch when they don't score goals?" asked little Jonny Piglet, who was a sports fan.

"Well, I don't know much about Trotterball, but not quite. The coach I got assigned didn't get to shout at me nor tell me what to do, and certainly didn't throw bottles of water in the air. These coaches would rather sit with you in an office and talk to you about things, usually what you want to improve," explained Edgard-the-Pig.

"Oh I see, so that was the secret. If I'm ever in trouble, I need to find this 'coach' and my problems will disappear… That sounds like the genie in the magic lamp of swineladdin," added Romy Piglet.

"Was the coach Blue and made funny jokes too?" laughed Jonny Piglet.

"Well, it's not that simple, piglets. In all truth, the coaching sessions were helpful, as they created a regular space for me to talk about what was in my mind with someone open to listen. And that helped me organise my thoughts and disconnect a bit. The main problem was that the sessions were too open-ended. My coach was always happy with any topic I wanted to discuss, so sometimes I talked about a movie I wanted to see and, at other times, about other subjects and projects I was doing. After a while, I just got tired. I started to find excuses to skip sessions and eventually stopped going altogether. I know this doesn't sound ideal but it was simply not adding value, and it worked better in the end," said Edgard-the-Pig.

"So, if coaching was not the secret, then which was it?" asked one of the piglets.

"By the time I started drifting from my coaching sessions, I found myself more connected with my classmates and steadily found that I had time to finish my assignments before evening, which had never happened before. Previously, I missed deadlines or simply handed them over incomplete. I cannot point out a particular moment or event, but gradually, things started to feel as if they were coming into place. And I started to enjoy University life. I even went to my first concert, Pork Floyd. What a beauty," said Edgard-the-Pig.

"Wow, Uncle Edgard, I wish I could go to a real concert with friends. My outings are still to watch Peppa Pig Live with Dad and the other dads," said Jonny Piglet.

"And we get to mock Dad when Daddy Pig comes to the stage. They are two peas in a pod," said cheeky Romy Piglet.

"That cannot be farthest from the truth, little rascals! Daddy Pig would dream of having the class and refinement that this magnanimous mammal has," affirmed Bruce-the-Pig.

"So, to finish the story, the second half of University was so much better. I got myself organised, with clear time boundaries to protect the things I liked to do with a real focus on those I had to do. I learned the structural components of building with Hay, Wood and Bricks. So I learned exactly what I should have done back then but learned how to work with more modern materials like steel, aluminium, glass, and titanium, which are all really exciting. My marks improved, and I got the Degree. I was officially an Architect," concluded Edgard.

"With Commendation!" added William-the-Pig. "That's my little brother!"

"And what is better? Not much after the degree ceremony, I got a letter from Pork Civil Corporation, the largest construction company in the world, offering me a job at the local branch in the Village," said Edgard-the-Pig, proudly.

"I heard they hire one pig for every billion applicants," said Bruce-the-Pig.

"That is quite an exaggeration, brother. The smudge has altered your common sense. There are not even that many pigs on this planet! Yet I give you that it was a difficult job to get, so cheers again for our little brother," said William-the-Pig.

"Yes, it was quite special," said Edgard. "I loved the company from the first day. Lots of talented pigs running things, dressed very smartly and speaking corporate lingo. It was odd at the start but I got the gist of it quite quickly. They assigned me specific tasks to review designs made by other architects, check some of the calculations, and do web research about materials that can be used for a particular project – all real projects, paid by clients, that would be transformed into real structures," added Edgard-the-Pig.

"And to finish the story, after some time, I got more and more projects and one day, my piggy manager called me to offer me a placement as there was a vacancy to run the sports division in London and manage a team. She had recommended me, so they offered me the job. Of course, I said yes on the spot, and here we are, celebrating our last dinner before I take the train tomorrow to London! I hope I can see Paddington Bear at the station so I can take a selfie with him to send to you, my Little Piglets," said Edgard-the-Pig excitedly.

"We will miss you, Uncle Edgard! Find a nice place so we can visit you sometime," said Romy Piglet.

"And I will miss you two, my fav piglets, and this family and the memories of this house," sighed Edgard-the-Pig.

Edgard departs ready to embrace his dreams

6 Human-Equivalent Months Before Opening Day

VI

The jazz music in the psychedelic pit was so soothing, and the face massage so uniquely relaxing that when the realisation of what was happening came, the sharp pain crushed Edgard's soul like a crumbling cracker. The massage was, in reality, a set of face slaps from a very tall pig in white, and the bright colours of the street lights of Pigtoria Street receded from him and from the bed he seemed to be lying on. The so-called music was the now so familiar tune of what in this conscious world is called an Ambulance.

His head was in terrible pain, and his body felt too weak to initiate any movement other than blinking.

"What happened to me?" He mumbled but got no answer. Maybe Edgard didn't even produce a real sound, or the metal clinking of the objects inside the moving ambulance impeded hearing.

"Oink! Oink!" he tried again, this time making a bigger effort. "Can you tell me where I am and what happened?"

The long-necked pig in white turned to Edgard and, in a rusty voice, said: "You are lucky to be alive Senor Pig. The Pork Stroke was quick, and you only passed out for a couple of minutes… You are on your way to the hospital for some tests and to start your recovery journey," one of the paramedics explained.

"WHAT?" gasped Edgard, "but WHY?" Then, like a flash, the image of him writing a resignation letter hit him, as it was his last conscious thought before the colourful cloudy trance took over.

Exhausted and overworked Edgard

VII

12 Human-Equivalent Months Before Opening Day

Architectural Tech Firms in the Pig World were the latest trend in a rapidly modernising animal society. Over a generation, mammals and rodents moved from foraging the forest for materials and running family DIY projects to building houses (over a tree or underground), pits or canopies, to using the swineternet for all sorts of aspects of their lives. Food could now be ordered online and delivered in minutes, shows and sports events could be watched on phones, and houses and construction projects could be viewed and planned online. Apps and companies like Pigterest, OINKEA and Uber Pigs were taking over and conquering the attention of the new generation of quadrupeds and bipeds alike.

In the new era of the construction world, Pork Civil Corporation (aka PCC) was the poster child of the future. They specialised in large and emblematic endeavours, mainly commercial but also real state and infrastructure, as well as fewer but state-of-the art residential installations. They were the first to build a Worm Planetarium, a sustainable free-range farm for chickens, and the emblematic Mud Lagoon Spa & Resort. There were rumours that rodent billionaires were having their burrows designed by some of the top architects at the "Corpo", as they are commonly called these days.

Every construction project is complex (especially those managed by PCC), with a large number of process steps and stakeholders to manage. To put it simply, there are four main areas:

1. **Schematics and Design.** It starts with the architect visiting the plot, engaging the client to understand the desired outcome, and bouncing some initial ideas to test appetite or reticence. It also involves creating the actual design mock-ups and the schematics of how basic systems will work in the new structure (electrical, plumbing, etc).

2. **Constructions and Permits.** This is where construction drawings are created and, more crucially, where the firm obtains permits from the authorities to build to specifications. It could be the stage that takes longer.

3. **Bidding and Negotiation.** PCC is a very successful company with a strong brand around innovation and avant-garde design, yet they don't have the capability for physical construction. This means they need a team to negotiate with third-party contractors to execute and bring the designs to life.

4. **Overarching Project Management.** This is the space where the deadlines, sequences, and milestones are managed to be delivered on time and with the expected quality. This would require transversal work with the other three departments.

The day Edgard met his team in person for the first time, it appeared to be very conventional, a classic Monday. The weather was gloomy, traffic was heavy, and animals were too busy to even say good morning in the elevator. Little did he know that he was at the start of a critical personal and professional juncture that would unfold in a number of unexpected ways, at least for him.

His manager Rita, who happened to be a very elegant bushy-tailed woodrat, awaited him with a small but symbolic welcome event. Cheese and carrot juice were catered and placed in the office lounge, which was full of office perks and freebies to entice employees to embrace the "cool quotient" of the modern office space. Rumour has it that it was a satellite office of FACEPORK, one of the top technology companies in the world at that time. So, when Edgard's company leased the space, they kept the furniture and decided to maintain the décor. When Edgard showed up at the reception for the first time, he felt a sense of positive insecurity since the vibe was new to him, but the opportunity ahead to familiarise himself with it made it quite exciting.

His new organisation would be a team of 30, all reporting to four team leaders who would report to Edgard-the-Pig: Bary-the-Badger leading Schematics & Design, Mary-the-Meerkat in charge of Constructions and Permits, Susan-the-Sloth heading Bidding and Negotiations, and Willy-the-Weasel at the top of his Project Management division. They had a healthy and diverse portfolio of projects in the south of London and central Manchester but none that had made a particular dent in Public Relations or captured public attention. A few restaurants in South Kensington and two residential parks in greater Manchester were their most notable works. This could have explained Edgard's terrified face when he heard about Project Blue.

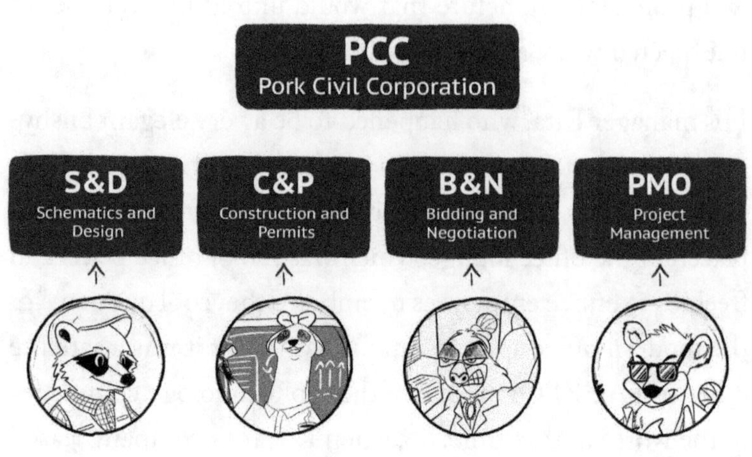

VIII

The mind of Bary-the-Badger was frequently wandering, hopping across times and places, real and imaginary, constantly creating shapes and stories. The memory of Bary's initial encounter with Edgard wasn't coincidentally tied to any specific words spoken (as Bary doesn't recall any), but rather to the image of Edgard's holiday residence in Bary's mind. Bary-the-Badger loved to play guessing animals' tastes and lifestyles from the first few seconds of interactions and body language and project that amalgamation of assumptions and signals into a holiday home. It made him relax and brought his natural anxiety levels down while creating an imaginary connection with the new person. The navy-blue scarf, round white glasses and khaki trousers that Edgard-the-Pig wore that day, combined with his rapid breathing and firm voice, created in Bary's mind an image of an art deco loft in Miami Beach with dolphin decorations inside. Bary-the-Badger was an artist by heart and reputation, with 20 human-equivalent years in the profession and ten at PCC, as well as three as the head of Schematics, a promotion he earned after having won the last Innovation Award for his Self-Sustained Bee-Hive using the vibration energy from the wings of its Buzzing Inhabitants. His creative drive was so intense that Bary's main challenge was embracing any process or structure going forward since he would perceive this as limiting, reductive and transactional. Deadlines were frequently missed and it was difficult to obtain status updates or simply have visibility of what was happening in his team. It made no difference whether a project took one month or three years to complete as long as the right outcome was delivered, one he could feel proud of and be able to look back at in the future and still spot no shortcomings.

Creative Bary-the-Badger

Unlike Bary-the-Badger, Mary-the-Meerkat could recall the words and pleasantries exchanged in that welcome event. Not only because her memory was sharp or photographic, as her friends would constantly refer to, but also because some key statements came when Edgard-the-Pig responded to the questions Mary raised. She was curious and eager to learn, very structured in thought and execution, generally introverted and the youngest of the leaders. She joined PCC directly after Meerkat University, where she finished a major in Civil Engineering (with Hons), and has not stopped developing her career since. She was recently appointed to lead Constructions in a well-deserved promotion granted directly by Rita-the-Woodrat herself. She is a high achiever with a contagious drive to deliver results and honour agreements, but she does not operate comfortably in environments of high ambiguity or company politics. She is very excited to finally have a leader and has very high hopes for the future.

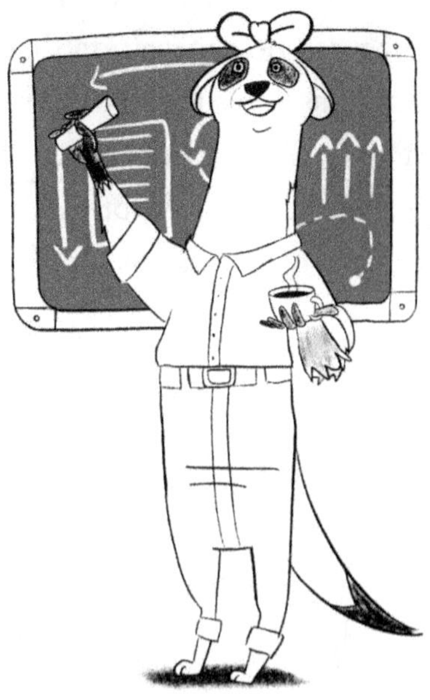

Over-eager, Mary-the-Meerkat

If we think about velocity to deliver change and agility to adapt, Susan-the-Sloth would not come to mind as a company representative. Actually, she wouldn't come to mind at all in anything related to commitment. She has been on the roles for the last ten human-equivalent years, and 25 in the company. She is an active member of the animal union, with flagship achievements in the corporation's early days, achieving for the first time the inclusion of Equal Pay, Flexible Working and Hunting-Free Holidays in all PCC employee contracts. She was well regarded as a specimen of altruism and philosophy, and she shared social events with the last five CEOs. Her track record at work, however, was less impressive, with a team constantly missing deadlines and holding the largest share of attrition and dissatisfaction of the firm. In Susan's world, a new manager was always a distraction, and she had no expectation that any meaningful change would come as a result, at least not one of which she would be a part. When Edgard-the-Pig finished his introductory speech, she felt a bit of fondness for him and wished he could last longer than the previous managers.

The Sloth's labyrinth

The last leader was of a very special kind. Willy-the-Weasel was the master of political manoeuvres. A true networker, proficient in conversation and small talk, business savvy and with an active social life, he had almost celebrity status in PCC (at least in his eyes). Willy joined PCC five human-equivalent years ago, straight into the Project Management role, and used it as his platform to build connections and influence. He had a reputation for lack of transparency and preferential treatment among projects and teams. Highly sensitive to status and social ladders, and in Mid-Weasel-Life, he remembers a highlight in his corporate life when he was given the car space in front of the canteen (apparently the most visible of all) so his Corvette Stingray could enjoy the spotlight and become the ice breaker in PCC conversations. He was eager to have the time to get to know Edgard better, to send him a nice present to his home, and plant the seed for a new salary raise conversation, hoping that the beach house in the French Riviera would still be patiently waiting for him to make an offer. That's why his memorable moment from that introductory meeting was the uncomfortable thought that now he wouldn't be the employee with the highest number of press articles and PR references since the golden child starring in the world-famous story of the Three Little Pigs had just joined the firm.

Willy-the-Weasel's aspirations

The meeting finally cemented the day in which Edgard-the-Pig met his new team and four new leaders – four peculiar and very different stories of behaviours, motivators and values that collectively would shape the future of the South London and Manchester division at PCC, and certainly Edgard's professional and personal life.

I later remembered the words that Edgard shared with his team that day and re-enacted them in my mind when I was preparing for a session. The speech was short, concise and full of enthusiasm. If only he knew what was coming.

IX

Regardless of whether you're a football enthusiast or not – though such individuals are scarce in London (and globally) these days – it's highly probable that you would identify the Chelsea Football team as a significant facet of the city's identity. Nestled in one of the most upscale and vibrant neighbourhoods, infused with the atmosphere of affluent individuals leading an easygoing yet opulent lifestyle, the Chelsea Football Club evolved into a focal point for ultra-rich owners, drawing in the crème de la crème of celebrity footballers. After many years of mid and bottom-table results, Chelsea's fame catapulted when the star coach-made-*socialite* Jose Porkinho led the team to win back-to-back championships with epic matches against the very best of his time. His love-or-hate personality made him a constant target of the tabloids and mass media and thus elevated the conversations from sports to celebrity gossip, which captured the imagination of youngsters and the middle class all around the country. Chelsea became not only the team to beat but the team to tattle on.

Today, Chelsea stands as an iconic household brand, spearheading the modernisation of traditional sports. It is prominently featured on the New York Stock Exchange and boasts an extensive fan base that spans across Asia, Africa, and South America, affirming its global resonance and influence. *Forrest Magazine* listed Chelsea as one of the top ten most influential brands in the world, and five of its players figured in their list of the 100 richest, with social media followers exceeding 1 billion among them.

In spite of the exponential growth of the fan base and their bottom line, their house stadium remained a nice neighbourhood-y space surrounded by residential buildings. Evening matches were not allowed as they would go against residential rules of noise control after 8 p.m., and capacity was among the smallest in the entire league. A charming field that worked for most of the team's history but was clearly not fit for purpose for this 21st-century sports behemoth.

That's why, when Edgard-the-Pig first heard about Project Blue, he was not surprised at all, and even thought that this idea had taken too long to become reality. Chelsea fans and stakeholders worldwide would be privileged to witness home matches in a state-of-the-art stadium – a venue designed not only to honour the traditions of the birthplace of football but also to redefine the future of the sport, offering an unparalleled experience for generations to come. The powerful parallel between Chelsea's history and PCC, his current employer, wasn't lost on him; hence, seeing these two journeys converging added an extra level of excitement.

The part that took longer for Edgard to register – in spite of it being obvious for the objective eye – was that the largest architectural project of the decade, and arguably in the century so far, was now in his remit, partly due to the location of the iconic stadium in South London and partly because there weren't many Division Leaders with Edgard's youth and drive. Hence, the fit was precise, at least on paper.

The expectations and visibility could not get higher, with a firm and a country's reputation at stake and a very steep learning curve to climb. Once he digested the briefing and reality hit at full extent, his anxiety morphed into executional energy, and he got cracking.

X

9 Human-Equivalent Months before Opening Day
Kick-Off Meeting Day

After investing three human-equivalent months in the role, completing various virtual trainings and introductory discussions, Edgard-the-Pig made a deliberate choice to fully immerse himself in the challenges of Project Blue. Recognising that this initiative held the potential to be the pivotal point in his career, it carried the weight of defining a distinct before-and-after era for the company's reputation. He called his four leaders to an offsite at Tree House Meeting Centre and blocked the day to share the fundamental structure of the basis of the project.

"Thanks all for coming. As you know, in nine months, we need to present a final design and project roadmap with costs and contracts negotiated so that a new Chelsea stadium can open before the new season starts. Timelines are supremely tight, so we need to make every minute count. I have crafted a master plan that I wanted to share with you," said Edgard-the-Pig with enthusiasm.

"Wait a second," says Bary-the-Badger, who was still going through his third serving of breakfast. "I thought we were going to brainstorm the materials and shapes we could use, or the utility purpose the design has to meet… I don't even like football and have the worst memories from when I was asked to play in elementary school. The least I need is to transfer that negative association into my design. Besides, a 'Master' Plan? A plan is already bad enough, but a Master Plan sounds Master Awful! Can we make it exciting, please?"

"Of course, Bary, we need to make sure the functionality is well understood, and you have the time and space to assess materials and structures. It should be captured in the plan. The intention is to reflect the different parts of the project and how they connect," replied Edgard.

"Yes, I like that," said Mary-the-Meerkat, conspicuously looking around at everyone in the room with her characteristic cognisance. "That way, I can start submitting the planning applications and notifying the council about elevations and subterranean parking lots. Let's master that plan!"

Susan-the-Sloth had taken so much time to adjust herself in the recliner chair that Edgard wasn't sure if she heard what he said in the first place, and was mentally getting ready to explain it all again. That's why he was surprised when he heard a mumbling laughter repeating the expression "*Supremely Tight*" as if it was the chorus of a catchy song.

"Mr Edgard," Susan-the-Sloth started with her typical parsimonious voice, "although I don't understand how you find it exciting watching a bunch of animals kicking a ball, I can tell this is important to you. You see, here we don't rush things, and we make sure that everybody is well informed and acquainted before we ask them to take action, especially if the deadlines are 'Supremely Tight' to use your words.

Surely, you can go back to whomever and inform them that a quality project needs proper time to brew, and if you rush it, you spoil it, and we are not in the business of spoiling dreams."

"But surely you would appreciate that a project of this size and budget requires careful planning and execution. We cannot just let it brew until we say it's ready," replied Edgard, now with a worried expression.

"Speaking about careful planning and execution," said Willy-the-Weasel while tightening his double Winsor Knot, "I like the spirit of the Master Plan, but we should call it something different, maybe the 'Perfectum Supplicium Protocol' a more catchy and refined term. I have already contacted the PR agency to start working on the press release. I'll reach out to my friend at the FiMammals Times to secure an interview and start generating buzz in the industry… so exciting."

"But if we don't have a concept or a plan how can this possibly help, and with what purpose? We have won the bidding process, and we are expected to deliver the project. There is no need to invest in awareness at this stage," replied Edgard-the-Pig to Willy's comments, but the Weasel didn't seem to react.

"Anyway," retorted Edgard with a change of tone and expression, "back to the Master Plan." And the pig opened a large parchment-like piece of paper with arrows, scribbles, notations and colours. There were so many colours that, from afar, resembled a scribble made by animal kids in kindergarten. The room filled resounding with Edgard's voice as he embarked on a monologue too technical to remember.

Despite the nods, the room was also filled with random thoughts from the leaders of the South London and Manchester divisions of the Pork Civil Corporation, who would rather be at the animal fun fair two blocks down than in that meeting that morning. And so the journey had officially kicked off.

It's like being back in school again!

XI

5 Human Equivalent Months Before Opening Day

"So Edgard, we know the journey, as you describe it, started with that kick-off meeting, and we know it led you here after a short stay in the hospital," I summarised.

"Well, that's a very simplistic summary, but I guess you are right," Edgard-the-Pig replied.

"Tell me what happened after. Actually, let's make it more interesting. Let's take one of your team leaders at a time and go through how your interactions with them evolved," I suggested.

"Ok, I hope you have enough time and a comfortable chair," Edgard pointed out.

Edgard-the-Pig began recounting the four stories.

XII-THE BADGER

Two weeks after the kick-off session, Edgard-the-Pig met Bary-the-Badger to discuss progress and become familiarised with the concepts. This would have been the first time he was not involved in the initial concepts, and he thought it would be only right to let Bary take the first pass. When he arrived, Bary-the-Badger was looking out of the window which faced the park, following a family of possums eating ice cream under a tree.

"Good morning, Bary," greeted Edgard. "Such a nice sunny morning. I am so excited to see the first concepts. Where do you have them?"

"Concepts? I don't know what you mean. No, no, no," said Bary-the-Badger with a big smile, "we should not rush the natural course. Those will come later. What I have here are some materials and shapes that I find fascinating."

He went to an improvised cabinet where he started pulling out strangely shaped pipes, joints, tiles and crystal-looking glasses.

"Last Friday, I was sitting here imagining the stadium of the future, when I got distracted by some brightness from the ground. When I looked in detail, I realised it was the reflection of the sunbeams projected over the roof of the ice cream parlour and back into this office, and as it went through the thick window glass, it created a prismatic effect on the roof. That was like an epiphany!" exclaimed Bary-the-Badger.

"Wait a minute," said Edgard-the-Pig, "I don't even know where to start. You don't have the concepts, you said? But we should have had them last Friday, so Mary-the-Meerkat can start her initial sourcing. And what does this sunbeam have to do with a football stadium?" asked Edgard-the-Pig, agitated.

"Exactly!" said Bary-the-Badger. "Nothing until now... but everything from now on. Are you familiar with a kaleidoscope, Edgard?"

"A Kaleidos-what?" asked Edgard-the-Pig in disbelief.

"K.a.l.e.i.d.o.s.c.o.p.e., Edgard. Pinkypedia will tell you that it is an optical instrument with two or more reflecting surfaces tilted to each other at an angle so that one or more objects on one end of these mirrors are shown as a regular symmetrical pattern when viewed from the other end, due to repeated reflection," explained Bary-the-Badger.

"I don't understand what you are saying, Bary, but whatever it is, I can assure you there weren't many in the pits of the village where I grew up," said Edgard-the-Pig.

"In simpler words, my dear Pig friend, it's the most magically symmetric pattern of colours and light you would have ever seen in your life, and most impressively, it's in constant change and rearrangement. There are infinite possibilities depending on the angle of the light and the objects inside," said Bary the Badger.

"Ok, hopefully, the punchline is coming," said Edgard-the-Pig.

Chelsea will have the first Kaleidoscopic Stadium in the world!

Edgard-the-Pig gasped.

"Just imagine, Edgard. The upper ring of the stadium will be reflective glass with large colour crystals inside that would be in constant movement as they are lifted by a column of pressurised air. The sun going through the glass will project the most amazing patterns onto the field, which will constantly change as airspeed changes or even better… Are you ready? As per the vibrations of the stadium caused by chanting and clapping. Every minute, there will be an art masterpiece on the ground. What a stroke of genius! Come on, admit it," added Bary-the-Badger proudly while making a gesture of smoking a pipe, looking more as if he held an imaginary banana.

"And I forgot to mention that the grass will be white, so these patterns would really blow the minds of the animal fans," Bary-the-Badger concluded.

Over-enthusiastic, Bary-the-Badger

Edgard-the-Pig took a very long breath and said, "Do you realise that players need to be able to see the ball, the referee and their own teammates, and that's one of the key reasons for teams having uniforms of different colours? If you add this festival of lanterns over them, not only will they not be able to distinguish anything, but the crowd will be confused over what is happening in the pitch. Football is not a fishpond screensaver, Bary; it's a game with clear objectives that require focus and preparation."

"I knew you were going to be a party pooper," said Bary-the-Badger, discouraged.

"I am just bringing basic common sense, Bary. Listen, I have to go to another meeting. Keep working on the concept, this time with a guardrail of having *zero* light reflection on the pitch, okay? I'll come back in three days, and we can take it from there," said Edgard-the-Pig, rushing out.

Three days later...

With the sudden exit, Edgard didn't register the "*Whatever*" mumbled from the other side of the room. Edgard-the-Pig showed up again in Bary's office, less enthusiastic this time but with the conviction that things would be in a good place, as he had been direct and assertive with Bary-the-Badger just days before. This time, Bary wasn't standing solemnly in front of the window or daydreaming in any other part of the room. He was actually on his computer, looking busy.

"Good morning, Bary. I hope you are having a good week," said Edgard, and then went on to ask him about the revised concepts, a bit apprehensive since he didn't see any sketches or blueprints anywhere, and the office looked unusually organised.

Bary-the-Badger removed his glasses and responded, "I heard your message loud and clear last time, Edgard. I took it that there was no place for my creativity in this project, so I consulted with a friend who recommended this new trendy concept of Degenerative AI, or something like that, to create concepts quickly. I have been playing around with it this morning, and it works very smoothly. You only need to give the Degenerated Robot a few hints of what you are after, and puff… you have a concept."

Bary-the-Badger types something on the keyboard.

"I mentioned that I needed to design a stadium in London with a capacity for 80,000 animals seated for football and concerts that can become iconic to the city and with some interesting features that could make it recognisable from afar. I pressed Enter, and Voila!" Bary moved the screen so Edgard could see it.

"You have to be joking, right?" asked Edgard-the-Pig, still unsure of what was happening.

"I know, right? Still not as impressive as my original design but if it does the job…." said Bary-the-Badger.

"That is Wembley Stadium, Bary. It looks very similar to THE Wembley Stadium which actually exists!" said Edgard-the-Pig, still in shock.

"And how am I supposed to know that? In any case, you can change the orientation of the arch or make it pink, and you have a winner!" exclaimed Bary-the-Badger.

"We are NOT building another Wembley Stadium, Bary! And even if we were, there is no way we would paint the arch pink," grunted Edgard-the-Pig, disheartened.

"Bary, just take the day off, okay?" said Edgard. "I'm sure we can sort something out next week."

Edgard-the-Pig went to his office, stopping at the coffee machine on his way and brewed the darkest sludge he had made in many years. He took all his drawing implements from his office cabinet and cleaned the desk, closed the door and played his concentration playlist in SporkyFy, and while he was getting ready for the first trace, he mumbled: "Looks like it's going to be an all-nighter… well, there always has to be one."

Edgard putting in long nights at work

XIII-THE MEERKAT

The day after Edgard met Bary-the-Badger to ask for the concepts, he set a time to meet Mary-the-Meerkat and get first impressions on the construction and permit work's progress. Edgard intentionally decided to hold his meeting at Mary's office. He finds it insightful and energetic to meet in other people's offices since there is a lot he can learn about the personality and values of the animal, or so he thought.

Just when Edgard-the-Pig was about to knock at the door, he could hear a voice saying, "Come in Edgard, finally you are here!" He found a very excited and pumped Mary standing in front of a whiteboard. Used coffee cups and scratches of used paper were all over the table.

"Good afternoon, Mary. Looks like someone has been working hard today," said Edgard-the-Pig.

"Hi, Edgard, just give me a minute while I write this down. I don't want to miss my train of thought," replied Mary-the-Meerkat. Edgard could see how the writing that started neatly at the top of the whiteboard was becoming almost ineligible at the bottom, and he wasn't sure if the scribble she was making on the wall (almost touching the floor) was in any known animal language.

"Okay, sure. Take your time," said Edgard-the-Pig, moving some of the notebooks to make space to sit.

"Perfect. It makes sense to take a break from it anyway," said Mary-the-Meerkat while moving another chair in front of Edgard-the-Pig.

"I just came to see how you were getting along, Mary. If you have any questions about the master plan or if there is anything I can help with," Edgard-the-Pig added kindly.

"Oh, yes, the master plan," said Mary, standing up and exploring the room with her eyes at her characteristic speed. "It was a good start, a basic foundation, alright. But not enough."

"What do you mean?" asked Edgard-the-Pig with curiosity.

"Don't take this the wrong way, Edgard. I thought it was too generic and gave room to conflicts and lack of ownership, so I built some complementary material." She then goes to the back of the room and pulls a rolling stand with a number of sheets.

"Here you see a Macro Plan for the strategic vision, a Micro Plan for each stakeholder, a Retro Plan for more details of the hours left before the delivery date, ah! A dietary plan for all the calories we will ingest in the journey and a Techno Music plan for the ambience, of course. I thought of a sleeping plan but it might be a bit too much, and we wouldn't be getting much anyway."

Edgard-the-Pig was about to start crying if he heard the word Plan again. After he gained some composure, he said, "Mary, at this stage, our main priority is to list and understand all the permits and the approval bodies that would be required and start making formal requisitions."

"Edgard, I'm confused," responded Mary-the-Meerkat, a bit frenetically. "All that is in exquisite detail in each of the plans."

"Yes, Mary, but have you done it?" asked Edgard-the-Pig.

"Well, no, because I have been busy building the plans, and I am a bit shy talking to strangers. In my family, I was always the last to get back into the Burrow when another animal approached us. Maybe I got some unresolved trauma," said Mary-the-Meerkat, making a mental note.

"Okay, Mary, you can do with some fresh air and a good rest to let all that caffeine dry out. Go home, and I'll see you tomorrow," said Edgard-the-Pig, knowing it was the right suggestion but fearing that there could be repercussions.

It was obvious to Edgard that for the sake of a good project start, he had to make all these calls and get those first requisitions through. He prepared himself for another all-nighter. The second in a row… *Must be bad luck*, he thought.

Tiredness begins to seep in

XIV-THE SLOTH

This was Edgard-the-Pig's third attempt to meet Susan-the-Sloth in person, or I should better say in animal. Twice, she had confirmed and cancelled at the last minute. The first time she was off sick, and the second, supposedly attending urgent meetings. Given her experience, half of Edgard was hoping she could be his right hand to drive the project to completion and earn the team's respect. The other half, however, was holding off from keeping hopes too high and was rather preparing for another set of worries.

When Edgard-the-Pig arrived at Susan's office, he found her quietly working by her desk and silently gave a little nudge to his optimistic half. They exchanged polite pleasantries and talked about the weather and how the tree canopies are becoming prohibitive to live, with inflation rising and deforestation reducing forest supply. Then, they turned away from the doom and gloom and got acquainted with each other's families, Edgard-the-Pig learned that the Sloth household was full with a partner and three little ones. When they finally got to the topic at hand, Edgard-the-Pig broke the ice.

"Susan, I know architectural design is not yet out, as well as license permits, but we should be ready to get hands-on with the construction when the time comes. Tell me, do we have a shortlisted set of companies vetted and within reach that we can mobilise?"

Susan responded with a very grave and parsimoniously slow voice, "Well, the honest answer is no, and it would follow that there is no point in acting now. We are still weeks away from having the designs and permissions. Come and visit then, and we can see what needs to happen."

"I thought that vetting and registering a builder as a new contractor would take time, and although we don't have the design yet, we can all be sure the project will be quite large, like nothing we had seen before, so we will need an army of potential contractors, plus any redundancy we want to add," The Pig pointed out, starting to worry.

"That's an interesting opinion, but moving ahead without confirmation that we can proceed and clarity of what we are building is like going into a large maze with no instruments. We could either face a dead-end or get lost in the process of trying to come out. I believe that my time is worth a lot, and if there is no design, I would prefer to dedicate it to improving the worker conditions in PCC, and make this an example for all the animal companies worldwide. We are close to unionizing the remaining two data sites that are not yet supported by the expert guidance and knowledge of Union Leaders. And since new elections are coming in six months, I need to be visible and plugged in with all that is going on," said Susan.

"Actually," continued Susan-the-Sloth, "I need to go now to our operation control centre with my comrade mammals, as we are in the middle of the photo ops for posters, flyers and all the swags for our campaign. You should join us, Edgard."

"Thank you, but I will have to respectfully decline. The biggest project of the decade is in our hands, as you know," said Edgard-the-Pig.

"It's your miss. Anyway, good luck and speak later." And she left in a rush, which for a Sloth means five minutes to get to the door versus seven for a Sloth at a normal pace.

"Oh dear," murmured Edgard. "It looks like Google and I will have a long night together. At least I can reach out to some of the biggest construction firms and try to arrange a future meeting and pre-book their capacity."

Another all-nighter loomed large.

Work continues late into the night

XV - THE WEASEL

The day Edgard-the-Pig met Bary-the-Badger expecting to see the concept for the first time, Edgard left the room in a hurry because he got a message from his assistant with the phrase, "Come to the office, quick." No context, just that.

While he was on his way, he checked his diary and remembered he had an appointment with Willy-the-Weasel, his Director of Project Management. His initial instinct was to call it off, assuming that he would need to take care of whatever was happening in his office. Edgard decided to wait until he knew more, and it was only a five-minute walk to the lift and down the corridor.

On his arrival, he could see a buzzing crowd gathered, not only because there were bees among them, but also several smartly dressed groups of rodents and mammals, as well as cameras, microphones, lights, and many cables in his office. In the centre of that frenzy, Willy-the-Weasel was handing out flyers and talking to some of them while Edgard's assistant Charlie-the-Chipmunk, visibly flustered, tried unsuccessfully to get Willy's attention.

Willy-the-Weasel was wearing a bright cream suit, with a light blue shirt and an orange tie, this time with a simple double knot, purposely loose at the neck to show off the golden button at the top of the shirt. His hair and whiskers had a wet and shiny look, and he was wearing rounded sunglasses, which, given all the lights, was a helpful accessory.

The shoes were not visible at first glance, but Edgard was sure they were equally unconventional.

When Willy saw Edgard enter the room, he extended his Weasel arm towards him, shouting: "Here is the Pig Himself. Edgard-the-Pig! So great to see you. We are getting ready to share the big news with the animal world."

All the journalists, reporters, assistants, podcasters, influencers and bees in the room turned and rushed nervously to turn their equipment on and get ready for what they thought would be a live *impromptu* Q&A, but they were disappointed when they saw Edgard's face turning red. He rushed Willy-the-Weasel to an adjacent room next to his office and closed the door. Since the offices were double-glazed and had noise-cancelling settings, the crowd couldn't understand what was happening inside.

"What do you think you are doing?" asked Edgard-the-Pig, furious.

"What do you mean? Sharing the news about our project, creating awareness and excitement. We are going to deliver the most futuristic project this city has seen for decades. Breaking the story now will give us leverage and help us gain allies to deliver it more smoothly," replied the Weasel with conviction.

"But we don't have a message to share beyond saying that we will deliver this project. We don't have a plan for which we all feel accountable, and I am also starting to worry about budget management after the unplanned event I see today," added Edgard-the-Pig.

"This is how we have done things in the past. To do my job well, I need to reach out to the community, and I have already secured so many followers that this event can help build even more reputational capital for the firm," replied Willy-the-Weasel.

"Willy, you are the director of Project Management, not of PR. You should be the one driving the project steps to ensure completion on time and within budget. Do you know that Mary has created a number of parallel plans, and she started to drive controls around them? Have you spoken to Bary about the status of the concepts? Or to Susan about the readiness of the builders that would execute?" Edgard enquired.

"Well, the important point is that everyone knows what they need to do, so I am not the micro-manager type, you know?" said Willy-the-Weasel, his voice faint.

"Have you, Willy? Please just answer yes or no," reiterated Edgard.

"No, I haven't," replied Willy, feeling uncomfortable.

"And have you built your plan yet? Do you know what the next milestone is if we want to stay on track for Opening Day?"

"Well, the thing is…" started the Weasel.

"HAVE YOU WILLY?" interrupted Edgard.

"No, Edgard, I haven't. The real truth is Edgard…" Willy-the-Weasel sat down and, taking a long breath, said, "I have never done a plan for such a big project, and I wouldn't even know where to start. My projects before have been small, and usually the team deliver their milestones, and I go and shout it to the world and pretend I know all about it. It usually works, but now with you coming here and asking so many questions and raising doubts… it gives me so much anxiety. I don't know what to do."

Edgard could see the reflection of watery eyes through his sunglasses.

This cannot be happening, Edgard-the-Pig thought to himself.

"Okay, Willy, you know what. We need to take it one step at a time. Go there and tell them that we won't be doing a live Q&A or a press conference. Instead, offer to send them a written press release that I will write later today. And go home, take the rest of the day off, and use it as a time to think about how we can move this forward," said Edgard-the-Pig, trying to be supportive.

"Really Edgard? Okay, that's much appreciated. I could take the Stingray for a polish then. And you know what? I didn't want to have the press release anyway. This project leader role might be too administrative for my taste. I will also reflect on that," said Willy-the-Weasel, peeved.

Here was another unplanned task that Edgard-the-Pig was taking on to compensate for his team, and he was forced to cancel another personal plan. At least he hoped this one wouldn't require an all-nighter. But it turned out it did.

Pulling another overnighter – poor Edgard!

XVI

The stories continued, as well as the all-nighters. The plans (or lack of) were further overdone or overlooked, and the sense of personal responsibility drove Edgard-the-Pig to invest more and more hours to compensate for his team. Finding time for a sit-down meal or even a shower became scarce – not that pigs shower too frequently, but they do eat a lot– unfolding a spiral of uncontrolled workload that worsened with time.

No wonder Edgard-the-Pig, the promising young architect who moved from the Forrest Village to one of the busiest cities in the world and was in charge of the architectural project of the decade, ended up in the hospital.

He recovered all right. After two weeks of complete isolation from work, on a nice cottage in his beloved countryside, next to a lovely muddy pond, and with plenty of time to think during the day, Edgard-the-Pig was ready to return to the ring.

It is now when I come in, and my story and Edgard's become one.

CHAPTER 3

From Academic Heights to Deliberate Coaching

XVII

My name is Albert, but sometimes I'm also called Albert-the-Owl. Yes, you guessed it: I am an Owl, more specifically a Northern Long-Eared Owl, or if you are among the scientific community, an Asio Otus, from the Strigidae Family and the Chordata Phylum. At least that's what my animal birth certificate said. I was born and raised in the forest of a land called Ireland, which is not very well known for any fellow animal figures but rather for green-hatted little humans hiding behind a rainbow with a pouch of gold. I have yet to see the first one though.

Unlike Edgard's, my childhood didn't have the flare of a celebrity upbringing. I was a normal bird with a standard life and standard friends. My family was kind of scientific and intellectual. My dad Isaac was a Great Grey Owl, a science researcher and for many years the chief director of the Large Falcon Collider, the LFC, the largest physics experiment in the animal world. My lovely mother, Rosalind, was a Snowy Owl with very fine features. She was an accomplished librarian, capable of remembering the titles and locations of thousands of books in the most prestigious libraries of the land, since she either worked or designed the cataloguing system for them. My little sister Henrietta, playful and attentive, grew up to become a well-renowned children's author with best-selling titles like *Owl Babies*, *Whobert Whover*, and *Owl Detective*.

I grew up as a shy and introverted Owl. Apparently, it took me a while to hoot my first words, and teachers struggled to get long sentences out of me. However, I always had an acute sense of reading other animals. I paid special attention to their body language, gesticulations, changes in tone of hooting voice and general vocabulary usage, forming an accurate perspective of what they were thinking or feeling.

I learned to interact with questions and attentive listening. Sometimes, an apparently banal assertion like "I noticed that you have arrived unusually late to school this week. Is everything ok?" could trigger an immense flow of emotions and information and spark a conversation that the other party would rate as useful or fluid, even though my interventions were short and interrogative. I learned that I was able to absorb and retain lots of information to create a visual image of the animals' emotional state at the time. This trait brought me deep friendships and relationships and kept me on a constant journey of self-discovery. This journey took me to college, where I got a major in Psychology (Hons), unsurprisingly following the path of comprehending the animal psyche to learn and release self-confidence and capabilities and unleash the untapped potential stored inside the imaginary shells each animal carries.

This degree led to more studies, including Masters and PhDs in Cognitive Science, Neurolinguistic Programming, Emotional Intelligence and Behavioural Science. They all kept me very busy and excited.

Yet the real passion was about to come. It was ignited by a good Bird friend who approached me for counselling and support. She was a very successful entrepreneur who had kickstarted many companies, releasing innovative products and services targeting marsupials around the world. Although the companies seemed to be taking a life of their own and she seemed to be doing well professionally and financially, she was feeling increasingly lonely as her decisions had led her to a life of isolation, travelling, and high pressure. We engaged in a series of reflective calls, where I mainly tried for her to identify the challenges and propose solutions. After six months of these sessions, she told me that her life had changed and that she was feeling "in control and with a brand-new perspective of life". To be honest, I was positively surprised and glad she acknowledged the transformation, but I reiterated that it was all her due, and thus, it was herself she should be grateful to. Her answer still resonates in my head: "Arthur, you should be a coach. You were born to do this."

Albert-the-Owl's Journey:
From Academic Heights to Deliberate Coaching

It was the first time I heard that word in a context that was not sports-related, so I wasn't sure what to make of it initially. I did some research as my owl mother was kind enough to point me to a number of books and places to get more information. I realised that coaching is a discipline in itself that looks to help individuals reach their potential. And that's exactly what I loved doing, without even knowing there was a formal name for it.

This realisation filled me with excitement. I then went to the next level, researched what was required to become a certified coach, and worked towards the corresponding degree. In the end, I was used to academic life, and the prospect of a new qualification was not a mental deterrent at all. On the contrary, I was getting used to the idea of continuing to develop intellectually in the journey to discover more about the mind. This particular degree I felt would have a stronger level of applicability and impact than all the others combined. To my surprise, I discovered that no referenced accreditation allowed me access to animals or institutions in need of this type of support. In other words, any animal could call themselves a coach. This discovery was exacerbated when I started searching for coaches' profiles and dug into their academic history and professional experience. I discovered a wide array of stories, most of them with barely a college degree. The unifier narrative was the reference to the 'Hours of Coaching Experience' as the quality factor to build credibility and not on the degree earned, which left me an aftertaste that I was Overqualified and Under-experienced to become a coach…

I persevered and registered as a member of the Professional Coaching Guild for Animals and Living Creatures, and since then, I have been working with many clients, most of them corporate, as part of their Talent Development Programmes. These were overall satisfactory but also were, at times, too open, with no real commitment from the individual to materialise a change, and matters discussed remained at a conversation level with no practical application.

However, the ones I enjoyed the most were sessions with highly energetic animals that reached out to me directly and brought their stories seeking guidance to overcome real or perceived obstacles. These ones came with upfront commitment, and where I could use my abilities as a coach to support the achievement of the goal. I called these *Deliberate Sessions* and, with time, adopted a more innovative approach, time-bound and focused on results, and called it *Deliberate Coaching*.

This was the seed of the Deliberate Coaching Practice, and it has grown since. With the motto of *"Dare to Unleash your Inner Potential"*, the practice now has professional animal practitioners in most of the largest forests and cities of the world and has contributed to making coaching accessible and attractive to every animal, not only to those supported by corporate talent programmes.

Unsure if it was attributed to the practice's reputation, word of mouth among the coachee community or simply because of the extensive social media and online coverage, but that Monday morning, I received a call that would open a new chapter for me.

XVIII

"Hi, this is Rita-the-Bushy-Tailed-Woodrat from Pork Civil Corporation. You are Albert-the-Owl, is that correct?" said the voice on the phone.

"Yes, Albert speaking," I replied.

"I will cut to the chase, Albert. I have been told you are the pioneer of this new trend called Deliberate Coaching. I need your services to work with one of our recently hired executives, who just went through a rough patch and needs to deliver a very important project for the firm. I was hoping you could work your magic to coach him to deliver this project. I need you to be the coach, and I am happy to give you a retainer equivalent to two years of work, even though we need the project in six months," Rita-the-Bushy-Tailed-Woodrat interjected.

"I appreciate your vote of confidence, Mrs Rita-the-Bushy-Tailed-Woodrat, but that's not the way this works. Coachees need to be matched to a coach on the basis of style, background and goals. They must be given the last word on selecting the coach and committing to this journey. I don't even know this animal, and neither does he know me," I replied, sounding slightly defensive.

"Let me stop you there. As per my research, there is no one in this Fauna with more experience or accreditations for the task at hand than you, and I am sure you have built it from working with many different styles, backgrounds and goals, so there is no question of a good fit. Whether he would voluntarily 'select' you and commit to the journey… well, you are also an experienced psychologist and behavioural scientist. I have no doubt that you have the cards to convince him. As I am sure you know by now, I am determined to make this happen, so trying to convince me otherwise will be futile," Rita-the-Bushy-Tailed-Woodrat added with determination.

"Tell me about your executive," I asked, trying to deflect the argument to a more productive space.

"His name is Edgard, Edgard-the-Pig. We recently hired him to run our South London and Manchester divisions at PCC. He comes with pristine academic and professional credentials, is a high achiever, and is an energetic and passionate animal. Three months into the role, we happened to win the largest bid the firm has made for a decade – the design and construction of an iconic football stadium. Given the location is in his geographical coverage zone, he was the natural leader to make this happen," described Rita-the-Bushy-Tailed-Woodrat.

"Go on," I prompted.

"The situation got unsavoury when Edgard got overworked and had a mental breakdown and ended up in the hospital," Rita added.

"I see. It was unexpected then?" I added with concern.

"Well, in all fairness, the project is massive, and he had only been for a few weeks in the Firm, and his team is not what we could call 'cohesive' for the lack of a better term… I think all these might have contributed. But the important point is that he is out of danger and recovering at home for one more week, when he will return to the office. I agreed with the doctors that a coaching programme was needed for him, and since the project still needs to be delivered, a Deliberate Coaching Programme is the best option," Rita explained.

"I suggest the following. I will visit Edgard at his place as a way of introduction so that we get to know each other. I will keep my right not to be his coach if I don't see us as a right fit after our meeting. Is that okay with you?" I asked.

"Deal, you will not regret it, I promise," Rita-the-Bushy-Tailed-Woodrat said, ending the call.

The Call of Coaching: A Deliberate Challenge for Albert-the-Owl

XIX

When I arrived at Edgards' place, I was unsure what to expect. I have been through a number of "forced" coaching situations where managers and organisations impose coaching programmes to comply with AR (Animal since we are not Human) requirements. Most of those didn't yield any great results and were time wasters for everyone involved. Every successful transformation requires the individual animal to want it passionately. Part of me was expecting to see the classical signs of arrogance, disbelief, and dissonance that many animals present in these cases so I could go back to Rita-the-Bushy-Tailed-Woodrat and justify my decision not to pursue this process. But that was not what I found.

I was received by a calm, mannered and educated hog.

"You must be Albert-the-Owl. It's a pleasure to meet you. Rita has already briefed me. I was looking forward to this meeting," he said, inviting me to take a seat.

"Likewise, Edgard. It's great to meet you," I reciprocated.

Edgard's place was a minimalist Nordic-style den with cream wallpaper and touches of wood all over, a large library full of art and design books and surrounded by the very pleasant smell of acorns. I could infer he was organised, with good design and colour taste, detail-oriented and intuitive. This positive first impression only grew bigger with time.

"Let me introduce myself properly, Edgard," I said after taking a seat, or more precisely, after standing on the seat. "My name is Albert-the-Owl. I lead a practice called Deliberate Coaching, and for many years, I have been working with animals from different species to help them achieve peak performance and transform some aspects of their lives. I take it that Rita-the-Bushy-Tailed-Woodrat briefed you about us connecting?"

"Yes Albert, she reached out and gave me a plethora of positive references about you. She is counting on this connection to work somehow for the company's sake," said Edgard-the-Pig.

"And what do you think?" I asked.

"I feel lost, but at least in a better place than last week when I was in the hospital. I would really like to believe that this will be the game changer, but I have been in coaching programmes in the past, and I don't think they work. On the other hand, I don't have much to lose, and I really want to create a success story," Edgard-the-Pig reflected.

"I see. Can you tell me more about those coaching experiences?" I enquired.

"They felt more like therapy. I remember endless conversations with no clear direction and practical takeaways. Since I always had a busy schedule, they got in the way of deep work. After a while, I learned to work around it and use it as time to not work, so I guess that was positive, but nothing else came of it. I also had different coaches throughout, and they were very distant. I don't think I even recall their names, to be honest," said Edgard-the-Pig.

"Thanks for sharing, Edgard. I can understand how frustrating this was," I said. "I have also been through similar experiences and frequently hear them from my coachees. That's exactly what prompted me to develop the Deliberate Coaching concept and practice," I explained.

"Interesting, please go on," said Edgard-the-Pig, leaning slightly forward.

"The clue is in the name: DELIBERATE. The programme is designed to target one goal, which we call the 'HEART', and in a series of sessions, usually four to six, we work to create the 'PULSE' and bring that goal to life. It's time-bound and intentional to deliver a quantifiable result. Throughout the journey, we define actions and gather insights that positively compound until we achieve the goal. The coach is a facilitator since it has to be your journey, but he is also engaged because the goal, once defined, is a joint goal. No more open-ended and therapy-like conversations, I promise," I assured him.

"I do like the sound of that," Edgard-the-Pig reflected out loud, and then asked: "Is there a limit to the goal? How big is too big?"

I replied, "Wonderful question, Edgard. The answer is easy: 'as big as you want it to be'. We will explore the goal in the first session and discuss these and many other elements, and hopefully, we will finish with a HEART that we believe we can reach and would feel passionate about walking the path to deliver it. Because that is the most important requirement of all – you will have to want it madly. What do you say?"

"I like to make a difference and know I have the skills and can find the passion to do it. How would the journey work?" Edgard-the-Pig asked with curiosity.

"We will meet for two hours every session, and you should use the time between sessions to reflect on the insights generated and deliberately act upon the actions we would have agreed upon before. The sessions will be conversational, and I will guide them, but basically, it is a dialogue between us. I would suggest to have the first session in my office. Would this work, Edgard?" I asked.

"Yes, let's do it, Albert. When can we have the first one?" Edgard-the-Pig asked enthusiastically.

"How about next Monday morning?" I suggested.

"Perfect, a Deliberate Deal, then. Thanks for coming over, and see you on Monday," Edgard added.

I remember leaving the meeting with a sense of enthusiasm and curiosity. Little did I know that ahead of me was the most thrilling transformational journey as a practice leader.

Deliberate Coaching Unveiled:
A Transformative Encounter at Albert's Den

CHAPTER 4

Deliberate Coaching in Action

XX

Session 1. Goals

When Edgard arrived at my office that early morning, I had already been up and working for two hours – which for an owl is a big commitment since we are nocturnal animals – partly preparing the session and doing my meditation morning routine. This would usually last 15 minutes and would be a mix of breathing, reflection on positive moments of the day before, and visualisation of expected positive outcomes for the day ahead. Given that us Owls are so attentive, it was easy to remove thoughts and get to a state of focus quite quickly.

Preparing for that session was a different aim altogether. I led dozens, if not hundreds, of Deliberate Coaching sessions with different animals and species – Pigs were one of my largest customer groups – and navigated through all kinds of animal journeys. This one, however, felt different. The passion that Edgard displayed in our meeting and the eagerness to prove himself to the animal world was of an intensity I hadn't seen before. By the same token, the size of the endeavour Edgard was tasked to deliver and the expectations from everyone around him were also uniquely high. The Deliberate Journey for Edgard-the-Pig had to be surgically framed and supported, as a lot was at stake.

And just when I was trying to reflect on the mix of anxiety and excitement that this new engagement was bringing for me, I heard the knock on the door.

"Come in," I hooted.

"Hello, Albert, it's good to see you," greeted Edgard. I could see how he took his time to familiarise himself with the room, scanning the bookshelf, desk, coffee table and the diplomas and certificates hanging on the wall. But it was a different piece of furniture that caught his attention.

"What is this cabinet? And those objects? It seems they all have some code words or random expressions. They must be important as they are in the centre of the room, and you put a special lighting effect over it," remarked Edgard-the-Pig.

"Try to guess," I encouraged.

"Well, I don't know, really. In the beginning, I thought there were spare parts of some sort or random pieces of stuff you store in case you need them one day with no real purpose. But then I saw the phrases and the lighting." Edgard pointed out.

"Ok, sounds like you are onto something. Read some of them aloud. Maybe that can help," I suggested.

"Ok, let's see: 'Sprinkly Sparkly Princess' on a dried mushroom, 'Pirates of the Rapsodians' on a chopped log… What does that say? Ah, 'Pony Walker' on a pebble. Honestly, they all feel so random," said Edgard.

"I call this my *Cabinet of Deliberate Achievements*. It gives me purpose because they were purposes that became reality and transformed animals' lives. Each represents a story so vivid that I get owl bumps every time I remember them. And with them in front of my desk, I remember them very often. They keep me grounded and constantly remind me what it is all about," I said while cleaning my glasses.

The cabinet of Deliberate Achievements

"But what do they mean, and why are they written over these strange objects?" Edgard asked.

"Well, my porcine friend, you are about to find out soon. Please have a seat and make yourself comfortable so that we can define the Heart of your Journey," I prompted.

"The Heart? Yes, I remember you briefly mentioned it when we met for the first time. I am intrigued though. What do you mean by that?" asked Edgard-the-Pig.

"We will crisply articulate your purpose, your centre, your goal… Are you ready?" I asked.

Edgard nodded in readiness.

"Perfect. We will go through a series of conversational questions. Please be as open and candid as you can. Here is a notebook. I call it the *Box of Insights*. This is for you to write anything you discover about yourself throughout this journey. You can choose to share some of that with me in our conversations or not; it is entirely up to you, but you must try to reflect on paper when you feel something is worth annotating." Albert handed the notebook over to Edgard.

"Ok, so Edgard, let me start with a simple one. What do you want?" asked Albert-the-Owl.

"I want a miracle." Edgard smiled.

"A miracle?" inquired Albert.

"Yes, sorry, I was being sarcastic. It's probably not the best way to start. I want to build a stadium for Chelsea FC in the next six months," said Edgard.

"Ok, tell me more," prodded Albert.

"It is the largest project ever managed by my company, and I have been appointed to lead it, which I take as a great vote of confidence, but I don't know if I have what it takes," hesitated Edgard-the-Pig.

"I see. Tell me something, Edgard, why do you want to build a stadium for Chelsea FC in the next six months?" asked Albert.

"Because that's what I have been asked to do," responded Edgard.

"Interesting. Let me ask you a few follow-up questions. What was a highlight for you in May 2021?" asked Albert.

"What? No idea. Spring Break in the Brown Lagoon? Or that one was 2019…" Edgard mumbled to himself.

"Have you eaten any celery since you started this project?" inquired Albert.

"What? No, what a random question!" exclaimed Edgard.

"Have you met Frankie yet?" persisted Albert.

"Now, this is becoming strange. I don't know anybody by that name," insisted Edgard.

"Don't be scared. I was being a bit playful. Let me give you some context. 19th May 2021 was the date when Chelsea won its second (and most recent) Champions League in Porto against the almighty Manchester City. The Champions League is the most prestigious football tournament in Europe, only for the best teams of the continent's top leagues," explained Albert-the-Owl.

Edgard looked at Albert attentively, and he continued, "Celery, Celery" was the opening line of a famous Chelsea Chant, and it was common to see fans throwing celery to the pitch in the celebrations. And Frank Lampard, sometimes called Frankie is the top historic goal scorer and an icon of Chelsea's heritage. Do you see where I am going with this, Edgard?" asked Albert-the-Owl.

"I think I do. I want to build a stadium for a football team that I don't know anything about. Or a sport I don't know anything about in that case." Edgard writes that in his Box of Insights.

"Now, Edgard, can you tell me what you think about the deadline of six months to deliver this project?" asked Albert.

"It is impossible and unrealistic. Even for a top performer team, this is the time it would take only to have the design ready, and even that is a stretch," said Edgard.

"Unrealistic, you said?" asked Albert.

"Totally. I have been trying to parallelise a lot of work, but honestly, I don't think it would be possible. My manager Rita set up the launch date, but it's not based on any plan, just the idea to have the structure completed before the fiscal year ends so that it can show in the right accounting plan," explained Edgard.

"I see. Is it okay if I play back to you the situation you are facing?" asked Albert.

"Of course, please do."

"What I am hearing then is that your goal is to build a stadium for a sport and team you don't particularly follow or care about in an unrealistic timeframe set by someone else without understanding what the project requires… Fair?" asked Albert-the-Owl.

Edgard takes a deep breath and follows with a very long exhale. "Yes, it is accurate. That seems to be the case." Edgard writes something in his notebook.

"May I share something I have noticed, Edgard?" Albert asked.

"Of course, Albert," replied Edgard.

"Thanks. When I asked what you wanted, you described an ask that somebody else gave you. Exploring this ask we landed on a place of general apprehension and difficulties. I want to try again and ask you, Edgard, what is it that YOU want?" explained Albert-the-Owl.

"That's a very good observation, Albert, and you are totally right. I have been obsessed with the task I was given and haven't properly thought about what I wanted to get from it," said Edgard.

Edgard makes some more annotations in his notebook, and after a few seconds, he continues, "What I want is to deliver something I can feel proud of."

"Close your eyes, and let's imagine you have done it. Tell me, what is happening around you? Who is with you, and what are they saying?" asked Albert.

"I can see animals in my village reading the news and my interviews in Bloomberg, feeling happy with the achievement and wanting to travel to London to visit the stadium. I can see my friends and neighbours calling my brothers to congratulate them for my achievement," shared Edgard.

"I am sure that must feel right. And what are the headlines of that news?" asked Albert.

"'The Prodigal Pig scores a major triumph for the Village. The talent of the Village Pig will be seen every Sunday by Chelsea fans worldwide when they enjoy their home team's performance!" Edgard's eyes brightened while saying these phrases.

"Prodigal, Triumph... Very powerful words!" exclaimed Albert.

"I felt I had to leave the Village to prove something, and I want to triumph to bring the joy back to them," said Edgard.

"And in your image of success, was it relevant how long it took to build the stadium?" asked Albert.

"Not at all," said Edgard.

"Excellent, so if we were to write a goal for our journey, our heart, the reason for being part of this journey, what would you say, Edgard?" asked Albert.

"I want to be recognised in my Village for building something that sparks entertainment and teamwork," said Edgard.

"Are there any particular celebrations in your Village?" asked Albert.

"Yes, the Spring Mud Festival. The Mayor hosts it, and all families gather for a week of activities and celebrations. It would be amazing to have public recognition there," said Edgard.

"Excellent, so should we target to be in Next Year's Festival?" asked Albert.

"Absolutely, and I think I will start approaching the Mayor with the news of what we intend to do here to pave the way," said Edgard.

"That is a brilliant idea! What else do you think you will do?" asked Albert.

"I will do proper research about Chelsea and go to home matches, join the fan club, and even get myself a Chelsea

Blue Jersey, although I don't know if they come in Pig Sizes," said Edgard.

"Fantastic! Anything else?" asked Albert.

"Yes, and I will have a serious conversation with Rita-the-Bushy-Tailed-Woodrat about the overall timing of the project. I need to agree on a challenging but realistic timeline to deliver this because I *will* deliver this," said Edgard confidently.

"Good for you, Edgard. Your enthusiasm is contagious! Ok, so let's summarise your goal. Tell me what you want," said Albert.

"I want to be recognised in the next Mud Spring Festival as the Prodigal Pig that builds a centre of joy and sportsmanship in the world. A Prodigal Triumph!" Edgard exclaims in excitement.

Albert smiles, "Now you know what your Deliberate Object is going to say. You just have to choose the object. What is it going to be, Edgard?"

"Isn't it obvious, Albert? A Leaf of Celery," Edgard says with a smile.

"What is my Deliberate Object going to be?"

XXI

Session 2

A month had passed since the day Edgard defined his HEART and expressed his commitment to bring it to life. I was pleased and very energised after that session. The goal was very ambitious, yet it was strongly connected to a personal meaning, and the inputs to deliver it were within Edgard's reach, provided that he put tons of energy and discipline behind it. Many years in this business had polished my instincts, and they were generally optimistic about Edgard. Ultimately, it was his journey, but as a Deliberate Coach, it was also on me to achieve the goal, now imprinted in the celery leaf sitting on my desk with the tag "Prodigal Triumph" next to it. It was a nice touch for Edgard to have sent it by rabbit courier ahead of the second session.

For this session, the preparation was more straightforward since the personal connection was stronger, and we had clearer avenues of work. I planned to explore the progress of the agreed-upon actions and ready prompts for visualisation of what is required next. I had taken a number of notes from the last interaction and logged them into our *Deliberate Journey Companion,* a tool which enabled me to access the insights written by Edgard and the goals and actions agreed upon.

I looked out the window and noticed the day was clear yet slightly breezy. Shortly after the clock marked 10, I heard the door opening, and a familiar face appeared.

"Edgard! Very good to see you," I said. Edgard seemed visibly more rested and might have even gained some weight. He was wearing sneakers and a classic khaki and cardigan combination.

"Hi Albert, likewise, it's good to be back. I can see the celery made its way safely to you. I was told to varnish it in resin to preserve it, plus it makes it shine and will be a success in your cabinet, I'm sure. By the way, why is it not in the cabinet?" Edgard asked, expecting its placement to be changed.

"The cabinet is reserved for goals achieved. It's on you to get it there. In the meantime, the celery will be cosy at my desk," I replied in an academic tone.

"Fair, I guess. I am not going to ask what happens to those that don't make it from the desk to the shelf," Edgard laughed.

"Hahaha, yes, better not. Fortunately, with me, there aren't too many of those," I said.

"What are we going to do today, Sensei Coach?" asked Edgard-the-Pig.

"You know, you can just call me Albert," I said and continued. "Well, since you asked, we are going to work on the 'PULSE' in this and the subsequent sessions. In the session last month, we defined the 'HEART,' which was your goal. We want to make your dream come true, so we need to give it a pulse. That will take the remaining sessions as this requires a number of achievements to connect all the relevant parts. It will be exciting."

"I like the sound of it. Let's sit and do it then," Edgard said.

"I suggest flying to the park next door; the day is nice, and some nature can be energising," I added.

"Well, last time I checked Pigs cannot fly. Not sure we can have a conversation while we move unless we use our headphones," Edgard said jokingly.

"You are totally right. I have been with many bird coachees lately and I have forgotten some of the logistical details. But guess what? I can walk too. So, let's head to that green world a few blocks from here, and we can talk about it," I said.

And we started walking and getting deeper into the session's dynamic.

A Deliberate Coaching session in the park

XXII

"Tell me about last month, Edgard, and the actions you took," asked Albert.

"I have so much to tell you, Albert. Let me start with the most time-pressing action. I had a very good conversation with Rita-the-Bushy-Tailed-Woodrat, my manager. I was very open with her and did my best to explain what the project needed and the unrealistic date we were targeting," explained Edgard.

"Good for you, Albert. How did she take it?"

"She was very resistant at the beginning and spoke about the commitment and the credibility as a company, etc. But I guess she realised that the option of a poor result could be irreversible reputational damage. At the same time, delays and delivery date adjustments happen all the time in this industry. I tried to reassure her that we would have a stretch date but one built from understanding the dependencies and the steps needed from all the teams involved. That way, we could manage the project properly and be able to act promptly when we get signals of deviation, said Edgard.

"It sounds very sensible, Edgard. Did you land on a new date, then?" asked Albert.

"We did indeed. We set it up for a year from now, anchoring on the first match of the Champions League next season. That's, of course, assuming that Chelsea would qualify, which

I have high confidence in given their performance this year," said Edgard confidently.

"Look at you, even having a perspective on Chelsea's chances for the Champions League… But hold that thought since that was another action from the last session. Tell me how this outcome and interaction with Rita made you feel?" asked Albert.

"Liberated, relieved, empowered. For the first time, I feel I am in control, and since I set the new delivery date based on my assessment of the risks and dependencies, I am 100% behind it. It was also great to see Rita responding well to my recommendations and making me feel like a true leader," said Edgard.

I made a mental note to discuss this interaction with Rita later.

"Well, Edgard, that is fantastic. Well done. Would you consider this action closed, then?" asked Albert.

"Absolutely. Done and passed with flying colours, and I marked it in the system as completed, which by the way, is super easy to use," said Edgard.

"I am glad to hear, and thanks for the feedback. Tell me about your other actions," said Albert.

"The easy one. I called my older brother Pig to help me set up a conference with the Mayor of the Village, and I got it. It was a very warm conversation, mostly remembering the old times and getting acquainted with the recent news about the Village animals. We discussed the Mud Festival and agreed to have a special presentation in the edition after the delivery date. There was no point in talking logistics with so much anticipation, so we agreed to reconnect in a few months," said Edgard.

"I can sense this was somewhat emotional for you." Albert pointed out.

"It was, although it was a straightforward call. It still resounds in my mind in a positive way. I made a deliberate commitment to my friends and family to deliver something, and I feel even more committed. I also feel inspired because I know how exciting it will be for the Village to be part of this project," said Edgard enthusiastically.

"Another action completed then. Make sure you also mark it together with the feeling and the insights from it. Anything else, Edgard?" asked Albert.

"Oh, pig hell yeah. The most difficult of the three actions. Becoming a worthy Chelsea Fan in a month," said Edgard.

"That's a very original way to characterise it. How did it go?" asked Albert.

"Let me tell you an anecdote first, and I promise I will get to your question. I realised I needed to rebuild trust with Bary-the-Badger. He is, after all, our master designer and a true artist. I was unhappy with how things ended last time between us. So, I had an open conversation with him, with no task or agenda other than talking things over and resetting our ways of working. We went to a cocktail bar he liked and over a couple of Salty Dogs (gin with grapefruit juice and a pinch of salt. Yes, I also increased my cocktail acumen), agreed to give it another try. I invited him to go to the next Chelsea match as a couple of animal friends and enjoy the Sunday afternoon," said Edgard.

"I am pleased to see this initiative, Edgard. It sounds like a great idea," said Albert.

"And it was a great day. Chelsea beat arch-rival Arsenal 3-0, fans were euphoric, and the match itself was non-stop action. I thought 90 minutes was a long time to watch animals running behind a ball, but I lost track of it and was surprised when the referee whistled the end of the game. It was very easy to understand the rules and even the tactics and who the better players were after some time. There were great goalkeepers' saves, yellow cards, penalty shots and even a couple of goals disallowed for something called VAR; it was all really exciting. Bary was visibly surprised at how much fun he had. When we left the stadium, he thanked me profusely. His words are still stuck in my head, 'We need to give these fans and this team a worthy place to celebrate their victories. You will get a design in two weeks," said Edgard.

"Thanks for sharing, Edgard. What do you make of this experience?" asked Albert-the-Owl.

"That animal beings are different in many ways but we all need to find purpose and meaning in what we do to make it as good as we possibly can. It was when Bary realised that he was not designing a structure but instead giving joy to fans when he felt motivated to do his task," explained Edgard.

"Very good insight, Edgard. Well done!" congratulated Albert.

"And that brings me to your earlier question. Yes, I attended this and watched all the other Chelsea matches on telly. I also watched the Champions League finals that Chelsea won and visited the Chelsea Museum at Sandford Bridge. I also got my away and home kit and am trying to learn the Celery song," said Edgard with a smile.

"Wow, we sure have a fan over here," laughed Albert.

"But I went beyond and also familiarised myself with the Premier League, FA Cup, UEFA and FIFA World Cups, since those are the big stages with Chelsea and their players are watched delivering their magic," said Edgard.

I could see the excitement and speed increasing as more ideas kept flowing.

"Did you know that many Premier League teams have animals in their names and logos? Chelsea has a rampant lion taken from the coat of arms of the Metropolitan Borough of Chelsea. But there are others. Tottenham's is a fighting cockerel. Crystal Palace is known as The Eagles, Leicester City as The Foxes, Liverpool has the mythical Liver Bird in its crest, Newcastle United has two seahorses, Brighton has Seagulls, and Brentford is represented by Bees. It's so amazing. How could I not have known this before? Ah, and you are going to love this, Albert. I even found there is a team in the Championships called Sheffield Wednesday which is called 'The Owls' and have an Owl in their crest!" exclaimed Edgard.

"Who would have known? Maybe I should support them! That sounds like an important milestone for your end goal, Edgard. Good for you," said Albert.

"Another hit to the list," said Edgard.

With that thought, Edgard and Albert arrived at the park, and they chose an old bench under a large Sycamore tree to sit and continue their conversation.

"Let's switch gears now to what we have ahead of us," said Albert.

XXIII

"What is happening at the moment, Edgard?" asked Albert.

"I am happy to be on the right track. The new timeline and alignment with Bary gave me breathing space. However, I think it is not enough," said Edgard honestly.

"How so?" asked Albert.

"The organisation is still fragile and not aligned. Even if we get a good design soon, I fear we will be bottlenecked with all the bidding and negotiations with potential construction partners. In other words, we can have the perfect design, but to build it, we will need this stage to function," said Edgard.

"What are the biggest challenges?" asked Albert.

"They have a name and a species: Susan-the-Sloth. She has been in the organisation for many years and built her career and influence through internal political support. No willingness, skills or capabilities whatsoever for what the project requires," said Edgard-the-Pig.

"What are your options?" asked Albert.

"I guess I could always try to be upfront and talk to her, setting the expectations straight and see if she would be at least in the mental space to embark on the journey," said Edgard.

"Okay, that's one. What else could be done?" asked Albert.

"I could remove her from her post and give the position temporarily at first to some other animal, maybe an emerging talent from her team." Edgard thinks out loud.

"Anything else?" asked Albert.

Edgard, after some reflection says, "There is the option of doing nothing and seeing if she would organically collaborate as she sees the other workstreams gaining momentum. At the end of the day, she has been in the company quite a long time and should know the importance of delivering results," said Edgard.

"What is your initial assessment of the options?" asked Albert.

"With so much at stake, to be honest, doing nothing is not an option, especially for the other team members with whom I would be working and expecting Deliberate Change," said Edgard.

"I can see you are embracing the Deliberate Spirit. Ok, what else?" asked Albert.

"My sense is that it will require a more drastic intervention," said Edgard.

"I hear you, so what will you do then?"

"I will have an honest conversation with her and offer her an opportunity to manage other projects, decoupling her from Project Blue while giving the post to someone from her team who would report to me for the project duration. Her team would still be in the lead from the optics, and she could spend more time on other commitments," suggested Edgard.

"What is the very first step?" asked Albert.

"I am putting time in her diary for tomorrow just now. Give me one minute," said Edgard, while setting the meeting in his phone.

"And while you are at it, I am making a note of the action we have agreed on. Anything else?" asked Albert.

"And, of course, I will need to have the design ready for the next time we meet, so I am also booking time with Bary to go through them," added Edgard.

"Would you like to wrap up the key actions and takeaways, please?" asked Albert-the-Owl.

"Good start. There is promising movement on design, but intervention is needed in construction. Key actions would be closing the design and empowering Susan's organisation (with or without her) to deliver." Edgard went over the key points one last time.

"Magnifico. See you in one month," said Albert.

Under the sycamore tree

XXIV

Session 3

A month had passed since the last Deliberate session with Edgard. The passage of time was reflected in the humid and cold air, and the occasional shower – typical of London's equinoxical seasons – which could have made a stroll in the park uncomfortable. We had agreed to do this session virtually since Edgard was on a business trip and was not keen to change the session to after his return. For me, it was perfectly fine as a coach, and even more so as a Deliberate Coach, I needed to be flexible and adaptable to the busy lives of our dear clients. I used to believe that coaching interactions could only blossom in face-to-face settings, where animals were close to express and register emotions and non-verbal language, but over time, I learned to incorporate technology to enable the same quality conversations. In some cases, it even opened new spaces since you could ask about the setting of the other animal, which was commonly their houses, and was an invitation to know more about the values of the interlocutor.

At 10 am, I could see that Edgard had joined the virtual room, with a nice bucolic background, in what looked like the British countryside. As an Owl, I have an acute sense of the countryside. I felt I had to break the ice by pointing that out.

"Good morning, Edgard. I hope you can see and hear me well. I can see the green landscape behind you. If I had to guess, I'd say it's somewhere in the Cotswolds, although I can't figure out if it's in the English or Welsh side. If I see it at night, I could probably tell you with precision," observed Albert.

"Good morning to you too, Albert. Yes, you are so right. The location is Wales. You have a very good eye," Edgard replied.

"And ears. Not in many places can you hear the chirping of Pochards, Coots, Buzzards and Red Kites," Albert added.

"Sometimes I forget we have different ways to perceive the world," Edgard remarked.

"That should be one of the most important maxims of Animal Nature, and I heard that is also true for humans. You should almost make this the header of your notebook. Speaking of which, tell me how you did with the actions you committed to last month?" asked Albert-the-Owl, directing the conversation to introduce the subject speedily.

"Not easy conversations, I must say, but I am feeling optimistic about how they unfolded," responded Edgard.

"Feeling Optimistic? Tell me more," encouraged Albert.

"Let me start with the most exciting part. We have officially applied for the Designs and Schematics! Oink, Oink! And I love them," added Edgard.

"This is great to hear, Edgard. It sounds as if it was a fundamental milestone to achieve your broader goal," said Albert.

"You bet. With the designs ready, we can open different workstreams and progress on many other fronts. Plus, it gives a sense of achievement since now every animal in the team knows what we are trying to build," said Edgard.

"I see. What do you think they will see when it's built?" asked Albert.

"The design is futuristic and avant-garde while at the same time realistic and cost-efficient. Bary did an amazing job! He kept some elements of the kaleidoscopic idea, but instead of reflecting inwards to the pitch, the same effects would be created in the stadium's surrounding ring. That way, birds and passing animals will know when there is an ongoing match, and the changing colours and intensity will reflect the emotions rising inside the stadium. And the touch I love is that the louder the cheer the 'bluer' the illumination will become. Brilliant. The structure will resemble a 'Tepui', majestic formations that rise over the clouds in the rainforest of Venezuela, a South American country, known for its top plateau surfaces. They are meant to be the oldest rocks on the planet and home to the world's most varied and untouched animal population. The stadium will be a sanctuary for football fans, of course, but also for any animal on earth with strong connections to their roots. That means there will be plenty of live vegetation and plants all over."

"That sounds very thoughtful indeed. I can tell you are very excited. What did you learn from this experience?" asked Albert.

"That I needed to recognise and elevate the talent of passionate team members. Bary was an artist and needed meaning. Working towards delivering an objective while providing space to let the creative juices flow can go together perfectly. I also learned that it is okay to give feedback as long as you are ready to receive some and act upon it. Once Bary and I talked over our differences in expectations and assumptions, we found a productive common ground from which we could build a great proposal," said Edgard.

"Wise words, Edgard. I hope you captured them all," said Albert.

"Absolutely, logged it in the system and in my thinking notepad," said Edgard-the-Pig.

"Very well, then one action that we can put to bed. I believe there was another meaningful commitment?" asked Albert.

"Indeed, Susan-the-Sloth," said Edgard.

"Tell me what happened," said Albert.

"I used some learnings from the experience with Bary-the-Badger. Instead of approaching her directly with a preconceived idea of what needed to be done, I allowed myself to get to know her more. I joined one of the Animal Union events she was heading. I have never been too fond of these since I have seen many cases where the needs of employees are used to gain political power, with no real change for the collective, while you see the leader's way of life change ostensibly. In many cases, organisations become less competitive and the culture more complacent, and that's when competitors and the market leapfrog them, which end in redundancies and shrinkage – the very same situation the union aimed to eliminate," said Edgard-the-Pig.

"I understand, Edgard. Please carry on," encouraged Albert.

"I went to this event, sat in the back and just listened. I have to say I learned so much about the organisation, about her and about me to a certain extent, given my apprehension with these gatherings," said Edgard.

"Interesting, tell me more," said Albert.

"Susan-the-Sloth was fluent and eloquent, speaking and gesticulating at a completely different speed from what I have seen at work. Her words resonated deeply in the crowd since she got constant positive reaffirmation and applause. PCC, it seems, had grown from being an entrepreneurial, innovative and socially responsible company to a large corporation, where approval processes took ages, and decision-makers were losing touch with reality, focusing on these large and symbolic flagship constructions but leaving aside the support for the average citizen, the urban dweller whose space, habitability and general social interactions were constrained by the advent of technology, crime rates and uncontrolled urbanisation. Susan was passionate about using design to foster community engagement, technology to bring neighbourhood safety and new projects to bring affordability and scalability for the average animal. She mentioned how these projects are now shelved because they lack the PR edgy factor," said Edgard-the-Pig.

Susan-the-Sloth transformed

Edgard paused for a few seconds to gather his thoughts and have a sip of water, then continued, "I decided to change my initial plan of having the direct conversation and allowed some reflection time. I left the convention a few minutes before the end and went to the office. Once there, I looked at the Project Pipeline and the projects we have decided not to fund in the past ten years. I was shocked and amazed to realise the facts were on Susan's side: Over 90% of the projects that had social integration as the main focus were deprioritised, and the ones that were set as active found other blockers later in the process that stopped their construction or placed them on hold. I noticed one that had been filed by Susan herself – entry-level architects usually do it – which was about creating a state-of-the-art community centre in a deprived area of Manchester called Project Kinship. It didn't get the approval from my predecessor to start bidding. I'd imagine a matter of budget, but I could see the Design and Permits were completed, and they were very good," stated Edgard.

Edgard could not hide his excitement. "Then I saw it all clearly like a lightning strike. I am sure you can guess what followed. I approached Susan-the-Sloth. We had the most amicable conversation ever; I shared with her the impact her presentation had on me and thanked her for the conviction and passion behind her ideas. She was the happiest of all animals on the planet when I offered her the opportunity to bring Project Kinship back to life under her leadership. She even got more excited when I suggested aiming for the same launch date as Project Blue and ensuring that the PR strategy included Kinship in the narrative, hoping that the extra awareness would bring additional funds and council support for the projects, and even make it a prototype for similar projects around the country. She thanked me warmly, and together, we agreed to nominate Paula-the-Parrot to lead Bidding and Negotiation for Project Blue, which came with the highest energy and a very conversational approach to things – very energising," Edgard-the-Pig shared enthusiastically.

"Good for you, Edgard. Is there anything else to add before we switch to the upcoming weeks?" asked Albert.

"Just to say that there are many insights from this experience; I have captured them all. The main one is to not take anything for granted until you get to know teammates better, especially their value system which drive their behaviours," said Edgard.

"That's very true." Albert paused to look at his notes. "I can sense we are closer to bringing PULSE to this HEART. Tell me what is happening now and how we could use this session," said Albert, opening his eyes wide.

"Thanks, Albert. With the design and a path for creating a healthy pipeline of contractors, I need to unblock the path to grant the permits and empower the overall project management. Once multiple teams start delivering and the schedule progresses, more interdependencies would need to be managed," said Edgard.

"If the ideal situation is 10, what number are you at now?" asked Albert.

"For these particular two areas, I would say I'm an 8 for one and 3 for the other," said Edgard.

"Why?" asked Albert.

"On the Permits, I feel that Mary-the-Meerkat is more than capable, and with some guidance, she can be effective, although there is always the risk that she will overwork it.

With the Project Management though, I am concerned since Willy-the-Weasel has shown he doesn't have experience, nor has he given signals that he has the right mental model to approach projects of this complexity," said Edgard, concerned.

"What could you do?" asked Albert.

"As we reflected in our last session, doing nothing and hoping for the best won't be an option for me. The two areas felt almost unbalanced, with one animal over-indexing in willingness and skill and the other under-indexing in both, at least on the surface. I want to consider merging the two areas and giving leadership to Mary-the-Meerkat. However, I wonder how this can impact Willy-the-Weasel since he is keen to be in the spotlight," said Edgard.

"Edgard, would it be okay if I share a perspective?" asked Albert.

"Of course, go ahead," responded Edgard.

"Thanks, Edgard. Sometimes, what your team members say they want is not necessarily what they need. Placing Willy in a position to drive a complex project so he can get the spotlight might not be what he needs, and it can backfire if the results are not there. He would be in the spotlight but for the wrong reasons. Can you think of a way in which he still attracts attention and adds value with a reduced scope?" asked Albert.

"You are right, Albert. Well, a Communication Manager and PR is needed as part of Project Blue. That's it! He can be the de-facto spokesperson of Project Blue, the Communication Officer, meaning that he would still need to be involved and understand what is happening with the project but would not drive the deliveries. He will focus on creating positive awareness for the firm, the team and the project," said Edgard-the-Pig.

"Ok, it sounds like you formed a plan. What will you do then?" asked Albert.

"I will meet Mary-the-Meerkat, inform her about her extending leadership role, and work with her to craft a comprehensive plan to hit the new delivery date. Then I will do the same with Willy-the-Weasel so he can start creating the charter of his new post and work on a handover plan with Mary," said Edgard.

"Fantastic, and when?" asked Albert.

"That will happen this week. By our next session, I should be able to reflect on meaningful progress in these two remaining workstreams," said Albert.

"That's a great summary to wrap up the session, Edgard. Even better that we are just in time, and you could do with a nice walk on the green carpet behind you," encouraged Albert.

"Sure, Albert. Speak then. Bye," said Edgard.

Both animals left the virtual room to immerse in their real ones separately, content for what felt like a fulfilling session.

XXV

Session 4

Owls are nocturnal animals. I find it amusing that humans call themselves Night Owls when they like to stay awake until late. A clear redundancy, of course, since the word "Owl" would be enough to convey the message, but they are humans, and sometimes they need to overexplain things. December is, therefore, a great month for us, when the festivities and family gatherings start. Maybe that is why I remember the fourth session with sheer joy.

This time we arranged to meet in-animal (we are not persons, remember), but not in my office, but in a restaurant. Edgard chose the place and sent the location to me, so when I was flying there, I noticed that I went over Stanford Bridge, the Chelsea Stadium (soon to be replaced by a new one). I remember thinking how thoughtful Edgard was.

Edgard-the-Pig was already there when I landed. The table was next to the window. I could tell this table was the best in the restaurant, and I could sense some level of attention when animals saw me arriving. Edgard was wearing a tweedy scarf and a Gatsby hat of the same material. Pigs were not particularly comfortable in cold weather but Edgard seemed to see it as a reason to bring out his knitwear, which he clearly enjoyed. That might have been why he never took holiday breaks to the Caribbean or any other tropical location. He looked more confident and self-aware than ever before and had a winning aura all around him. I noticed he was reading a newspaper of an unfamiliar name. Still on paper for some reason. I thought there weren't many of those left.

From the restaurant, one could see the upper structure of the stadium. There was no match that evening but that didn't stop me imagining how busy this place was when there was. After exchanging greetings, I joined Edgard-the-Pig at the table.

"I wonder why you chose this restaurant, and particularly this table," said Albert with some irony.

"I was in the neighbourhood. You know how it goes…" Edgard replied.

"I am sure you were. You seem to have grown fond of this neighbourhood lately," Albert added.

"Look at the people around you, Albert. They believe they are happy, but they don't know how much happier they will be in a year from now. You see, this area will transform. The old stadium will still be there, probably the home of a championship or third division team, but just five blocks away, there will be a new architectural wonder, a crown jewel, a new stamp in the post office collection, a new postcard for London souvenir shops. And it will be packed with retail shops and animal entertainment like you haven't seen before. Maybe you should move to Chelsea, Albert," Edgard said.

I smiled and then added: "I think it will take more than a Deliberate Coaching practice for me to afford it, but I like the idea. And maybe you can design my new tree house too. I mean, since we are talking dreams here, and you seem to be very generous and optimistic today," Albert joked.

"I think that would be a great project to drive, Albert. I'll add a very large library and blackout curtains so you can enjoy your nocturnal vibe," Edgard said.

"And you will have a happy customer indeed…. And on that note, why don't we order some plates to share and start our session," Albert suggested.

"I have already ordered. You will not believe how good the cauliflower is!" remarked Edgard.

The celebratory meal

XXVI

"Why don't we start by recapping the previous session's actions as usual? Will you do the honours?" asked Albert.

"I meant to give the Project Management ownership to Mary-the-Meerkat and transfer Willy-the-Weasel to a different and more suitable role," said Edgard.

"Yes, that's what I recall as well. Tell me how that went," encouraged Albert.

"Honestly, it couldn't have gone better. Mary was over the moon with the new responsibilities and immediately cracked on. She adjusted the plan and created a steering group with functional experts from each area and a risk assessment cobra team, mainly with accountants, to work on budget controllership at a very granular level. She also informed the division's team members of the new structure. She set up one-to-ones with all functional leaders to explain the plan, ask for additional input and answer any questions. You should have seen her, Albert; she was a natural. Not that I ever doubted it. This assignment gave her the stretch she needed to grow her self-confidence," said Edgard.

"You are starting to sound like a Deliberate Coach yourself," said Albert.

"Probably I should work for you after Project Blue is completed," quipped Edgard.

"I'm sure we can find a vacancy somewhere… What about Willy-the-Weasel?" asked Albert.

"The conversation with Willy was difficult at first since he took it as a demotion in the first reaction. However, as we began envisioning the new role, considering the value it could contribute to the project, along with the prospect of reducing stressful hours spent on milestone reviews, it sparked enthusiasm and he wholeheartedly embraced the idea. He prepared a communication plan and a press release that he started seeding in key media outlets, outlining the plan and giving 'teasers' of the design without giving too much away. He started collecting testimonials from the fans, the community, and employees. He did an amazing piece with Boa Constructor, the Master Builder in charge of the project on the ground when the foundation stone was placed a couple of months ago. You might have seen it in the news," said Edgard.

"Good to hear, Edgard. So, what's next?" asked Albert.

"Actually, now it's about execution. All parts are in place, well-aligned, and focused on the task at hand. We are on track to complete the project and be ready for the inaugural Champions League match. Willy the Weasel heard from the club owners that they are trying to secure the Animal Queen and a couple of celebrities to do the opening honours. But that's one for worrying later," said Edgard.

"What about the Mud Festival?" asked Albert.

At that point, the octopus waiter arrived at the table with an iced bottle of champagne, two glasses, and six different shared tapas (Albert could see how tentacles help for this job). Owls normally struggle with fizzy drinks, but he acquired a taste for sparkling water since he was little and thought he would be perfectly fine. Albert also noticed animals walking and flying outside the restaurant, slowing their pace to peek inside, some even taking pictures.

Albert's brief day-dreaming was interrupted by the pop of the cork and the waiter saying, "Champagne is on the house, Mr Edgard."

"Wow, this feels like a celebration!" exclaimed Albert.

"And that's how it should feel because that's exactly what it is! And the bubbly could not have arrived at a better time," exclaimed Edgard-the-Pig.

Almost automatically, as soon as Edgard said that, I turned my gaze to the newspaper he was reading before I arrived. It took me a while to process it and realise it wasn't a prank or a rare coincidence. On the front page, there was a familiar porcine face with a big smile, wearing glasses, a stylish turtleneck (which should have a different name for pigs) and standing next to a miniature model of some beautiful and geometrically curved and colourful shape, that resembled…. A STADIUM!

The paper's name was *The Villager*, and the headline on the front page read:

𝔄 𝔓𝔯𝔬𝔡𝔦𝔤𝔞𝔩 𝔗𝔯𝔦𝔲𝔪𝔭𝔥

Home-grown celebrity and Maestro Architect Edgard-the-Pig unveils the plan for the New Chelsea Stadium at the Annual Mud Festival

Featured on the front cover

Albert-the-Owl was speechless and filled with joy. Of course, he had seen many goals become reality in the past, but this one caught him completely off-guard. He was somehow expecting further developments, and was not counting on it to be so literally similar to how it was imagined. It was clearly a lesson for him as well.

Albert also noticed that Edgard had a bag with other newspapers, which he handed over for him to browse. Albert noticed *The Times*, *the Financial Times*, *the Guardian*, and even the *Sun* had a story of the new Chelsea stadium revealed on their front pages. In spite of all the circulation and reputation of these magazines, Edgard seemed to treasure *The Villager* over the rest.

Have you read the news today?

"By the look on your face, I can tell you haven't seen or read the news today," observed Edgard.

"I am sure you are about to fill me in," Albert smiled.

"We did it, Albert! Remember, I told you how brilliant Willy-the-Weasel was in managing the media and organising events? He suggested creating a large PR event to unveil the new plan for the Stadium. Now that the design was completed, permits were issued, construction started, and Mary had a good grasp on the project plan, It felt like the right time to create excitement and bring as much support and attention as possible. Since I was clear on my goal, it was an obvious option to do it at the Village during the Mud Festival opening, which was yesterday. I know we originally conceived the recognition to happen after the project was finished, but I reckoned that this would be even more powerful since this is to have millions of animal fans dreaming about the future instead of padding for a job well done in the past," said Edgard, brimming with excitement.

"I cannot agree more, Edgard," said Albert.

"I don't have words to describe the day, Albert. It was pure magic. Never in the past had the Village had so many visitors. All mass media channels from around the world were there, and they took the opportunity to do special profiles of the town, interviewing villagers and my family and enquiring about my childhood and the pride of having placed the Village on the sporting map. I signed an exclusive with Hog Sports and PETFLIX to do a documentary, and they will follow me from now until the grand opening. Actually, say hi to the camera at the table behind. That's them," said Edgard.

Since Owls can turn their heads up to 270°, turning it 180° to look at the crew was an easy task. I waved with some mix of incredulity and joy.

"Ok, then it sounds like there is not much to do for the Deliberate Journey. The goal has been accomplished, you are in good health and spirit, the project is well underway, and you are on the way to becoming a streaming superstar!" exclaimed Albert-the-Owl.

"All thanks to you, my flying and nocturnal intellectual friend," said Edgard.

"I am flattered you think this way. I was only an enabler. The power for this transformation has been inside you all this time. What are your key insights?" asked Albert.

"I knew you were going to ask that and start going all coachy-coachy with me. Hence, I summarised it all here." He hands Albert an envelope. "Please read it when you are flying back or in your office. I would like this to be a dinner between animal friends. Let's relax and savour the moment and the delicious meal PETFLIX is providing us. Wave and smile again," said Edgard-the-Pig.

XXVII

I must have lost track of time, maybe the effect of the grape-flavoured sparkling water when I noticed we – and the table behind, of course– were the last animals left. I signalled to Edgard that it was a good time to leave, not without agreeing to meet again soon. I grabbed the envelope and flew back home (a bit erratically though), making a mental note to pop by the office the following day to place the golden celery in the Cabinet of Deliberate Achievements, its well-earned location. The evening was dark and cold, an Owl-Favourite, and I found it a perfect setting to open the envelope and read the List of Insights from Edgard's Deliberate Journey, which became my journey too.

XXVIII

HAY PIGGY DESIGNS THE CHELSEA STADIUM BOX OF INSIGHTS from MY DELIBERATE JOURNEY

By Edgard-the-Pig

1. It's okay to feel Positive Insecurity: Come out of your comfort zone but with a positive attitude to embrace them.

2. Familiarise yourself with your task. Learn the history, the context, and the anecdotes, and make it a familiar territory. Become a Chelsea Fan for your future projects.

3. Look beyond the task and discover the emotion.

4. Animal beings are different in many ways but we all need to find purpose and meaning in what we do to make it as good as we possibly can.

5. Animals and human beings have different ways of perceiving the world.

6. It is okay to give feedback as long as you are ready to receive some and act upon it.

7. Avoid making assumptions about anything until you gain a deeper understanding of the other individual, particularly regarding the foundational values that shape their behaviours.

8. Break a lion into small little kittens. When a problem seems insurmountable, break it down into manageable parts.

9. Behaviours are manifestations of values. To change the former, we must understand the latter.
10. Our role as managers is to unleash the potential of our teams so they can be the best they can be.
11. To lead it is to serve. You need to work hand-in-hand with your team and understand what they do (and be capable of doing it) if you want them to follow you.
12. Listen actively and observe non-verbal cues. The world communicates in many different ways.
13. Pigs and Owls can have lots in common, except sleeping patterns.

Big moments are shared with friends and family. See you at the Inaugural Game!

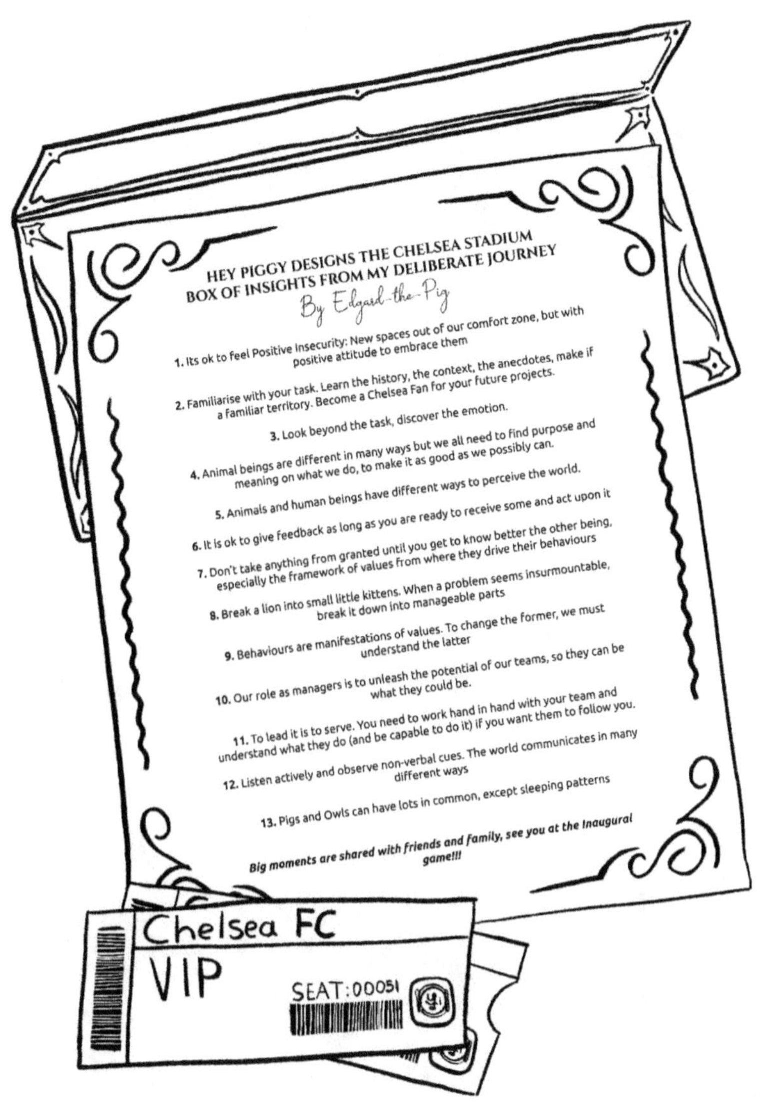

Two tickets for the match!

Epilogue

I can't believe six months have passed since our last encounter. I have so many thoughts and emotions now that it's hard to pinpoint which is the most surreal. It could be that I, a sport-apprehensive Owl, have been eager for the football session to start, or it could be that the Animal Queen and Prime Minister are more charming in real life than on TV and definitely better looking, or that the view and surrounding sound from the Royal Box is the most spectacular experience ever, or that I am about to witness history when the referee whistles in a few moments. Or all of them together, for that matter.

I can also see Edgard-the-Pig and his family enjoying themselves, including his two adorable little nephews wearing giant blue hats. His older brothers are here too, and it's not difficult to notice the pride and sheer happiness in their eyes, which turned into tears when they witnessed the official stadium inauguration, with the Queen cutting the ribbon and Edgard delivering a marvellous speech. It's interesting to see the paradoxical power of families that create limitations for some members, and those limitations are precisely the drivers that make the change possible. I can also see other animals in the box, and from the photos and news coverage, I recognise Willy-the-Weasel, wearing a shiny light-blue suit, pointy sunglasses and a curly fringe matching waxed whiskers. Next to him, Mary-the-Meerkat sits with a big smile and a very large box of tortilla chips, and waves at me for the sixth time in the last ten minutes, and to pretty much every other person in the royal box. Next is Bary-the-Badger, with his round yellow glasses and very visible orange tracksuit, watching the pitch in profound contemplation as if seeing through the grass. I couldn't stop thinking about him on my way to the stadium. His kaleidoscopic idea created such luminosity that I felt I was going underwater, through a waterfall or the end of a rainbow, and when I entered the stadium, the contrast with the bright green pitch created a truly perplexing effect. Next to me is Rita the Bushy-Tailed Woodrat, with whom I became acquainted after the Deliberate Journey ended. Animals say we make an interesting couple, and I could not agree more!

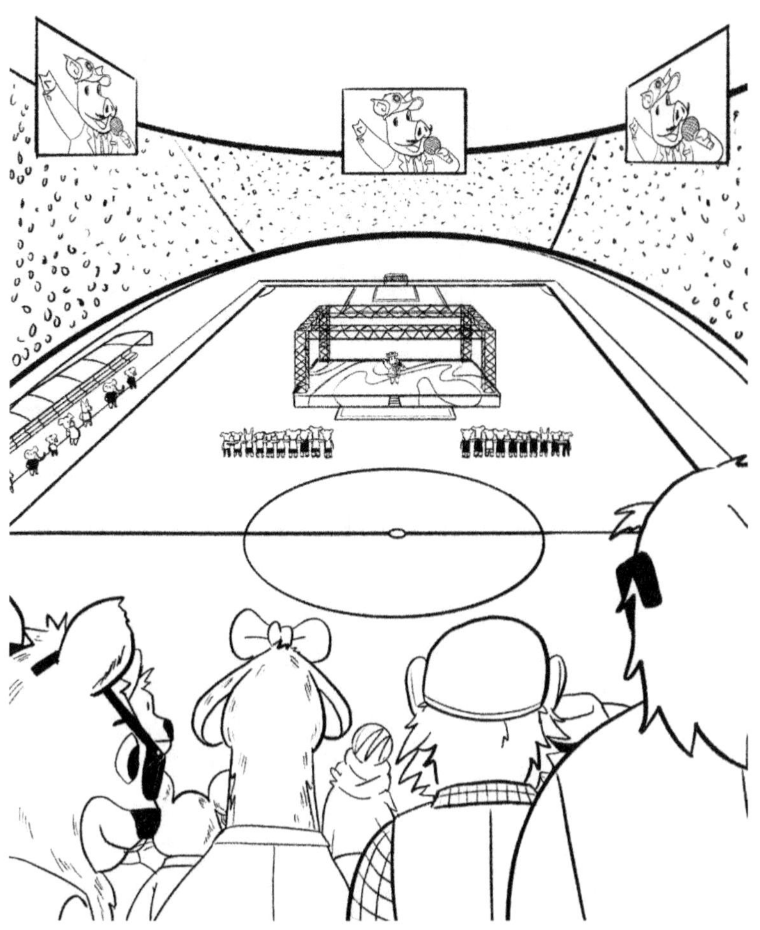

Edgard-the-pig's triumphant speech

And just like that, the whistle blows, and the match starts.
TWIT-TWOO Chelsea!

PART3

Dissecting How Little Piggy Designs the Chelsea Stadium (Spoiler Alert)

By now, you have observed Edgard-the-Pig's transformative journey as he steps into a new professional era, adopting a fresh approach to work and, in the process, impacting not only the lives of those around him but also his own. Similarly, you have read and imagined how Albert-the-Owl used his coaching skills to enable this transformation. We hope you were able to recognise some of the elements of Deliberate Coaching as the story unfolded, and smiled occasionally while reading through the pages.

The purpose of this section is to reflect on the elements of the story and its connection with the Deliberate Model.

THE CHARACTERS: ANY RESEMBLANCE TO REALITY IS PURE COINCIDENCE... OR NOT

Although framed in the animal world, the elements of the story are familiar in the human and professional world. Our main character is Edgard, a young manager with bright potential who is given a bigger scope and a large platform, surrounded by ambiguity and a number of 'NEWS': New team, new manager, new city, new company and new project. This happens at a fast pace, while Edgard, insecure and an overachiever, tries to make sense of this new reality and adjust his inner core. The situation Edgard went through aims to reflect the entirety of what many professionals have and continue facing: Change, anxiety, and low self-confidence.

On the other side of the fence sits our star coach, Albert, represented by an Owl given the introspective and attentive traits attached to these animals. The story portrays his professional trajectory and how he moved from general to Deliberate Coaching, outlining the benefits behind the approach: Joint accountability to drive tangible results in a specific time period. He sets the pace and approach to take Edgard through the HEART and PULSE until the goal is finally achieved. He prepares, thinks deeply about the sessions and aims to bring his best self into the Coaching Instances.

Apart from Edgard and Albert, the narrative introduces several characters who, to varying extents, directly influence the Deliberate Journey. Since the main source of ambiguity and expectation comes from the situation instigated by the role changes, the most influential characters are at the workplace.

Edgard's manager, Rita, is very direct and influential, determined to deliver commitments and not take no for an answer. She serves as the catalyst for perceived high expectations and anxiety related to failure by setting clear expectations for outcomes but not actively participating in resolving issues or generating ideas for a solution. At the same time, she acts as a facilitator, providing support for Edgard's turnaround when the situation becomes critical. She commissions Albert to work with Edgard. Although fictitious and one-dimensional at times, it is common to find elements of Rita in modern managers, who provide directions on what is expected or what to do but do not get involved again until it's too late or the project has reached a critical point, by which time the approach to turnaround usually brings stress and amplifies the anxiety. The turnaround was palpable in the story, yet it doesn't happen like that in all cases.

Edgard's team leaders bring dimensions of diversity and styles that are commonly found in the workplace. In all cases, Edgard grapples with the contrast between his perception of the right approach and how it is viewed from the leader's perspective, often encountering significant differences. In all situations, Edgard has to go deeper and get to know the person (or animal) better and understand their values and mental frameworks. It is only there that the common ground emerges, and the construction really begins. This is an essential part of situational leadership and the main challenge in Edgard's Deliberate Journey. He needs to deliver through others, so he needs to act as the situational leader who will make that possible. The Deliberate Instances are narrated in alignment with project stages and characters, ensuring the management and successful advancement of every session. While real Deliberate Journeys may not strictly follow this linear approach, the core concept of breaking down the goal into attainable milestones remains highly valuable.

The first leader Bary, portrayed as a Badger, exemplifies the paradoxical challenge of "Taming Creativity". On one hand, there is a very creative professional with a particular way of approaching problems and delivering results, on the other hand, the project manager in Edgard requires structure and certainty and needs to deliver milestones on time to unlock the rest of the workstreams. After a number of frustrating interactions for both parts, Edgard finds a way to achieve a creative solution with high energy and on time in the Deliberate Model. This takes investment in building a relationship, getting closer to the customer and connecting at a more personal level.

The second leader Mary, portrayed as a Meerkat, brings almost the opposite style of Bary. Young, talented and eager to leave a legacy, Mary needs to be given the opportunity and platform to shine. However, this is not straightforward, as she is dependent on Bary's work output and that of other leaders. The challenge is harnessing the great in Mary while keeping her motivation high and protecting her from burning out. Again, this is a common situation that managers face when dealing with low-experience and high-potential profiles.

The third leader is Susan, over-indexing in experience and organisational knowledge, she is a custodian of tribal knowledge and anecdotes that have shaped the company culture, and is highly respected among a large number of employees for her conviction for a cause. On the project at hand, however, she is sceptical from the start, passively at first, and actively later, instigating friction all along. Susan represents the organisational characters who "have seen it all", the voice of the status quo, the "this has always been like this, so why change it". With little experience and high eagerness, Edgard has to find a way to overcome such a strong power of influence and get her at least to a neutral position, enabling him to move the project forward. He again invests in deep diving into her values and learning to appreciate what she brings and respect what she stands for, and in doing so, discovers there is a place for both within the larger project. In areas with strong employee unions or representation, Susan resonates as a beacon of justice and equality and thus pulls appreciation from the employees.

The final leader, Willy, also has a unique profile. At the surface, he represents the social media generation, creating his digital persona in search of recognition and instant gratification to achieve material rewards that could be showcased, thus feeding the vicious cycle. In reality, Willy is insecure and underprepared for the challenges Edgard needs.

He is not used to hard work or long-term and sustainable gratification. Willy is arguably the character that poses the largest challenge for Edgard as a leader, not only because he finds it difficult to find a fit for the project at hand but also because of the most profound thought that Willy represents a new generation that was shaped by the modern world and the existing organisational culture. I am sure you would recognise some of these workplace characteristics, which are arguably more accentuated in technology and digital-heavy industries. After a series of setbacks, Edgard manages to create the conditions for a positive settlement, reflecting the thought leadership and influencing needed in these situations.

In the family, the characters offer a perspective of how "familiar" and "safe" environments with trust and love are also sources of anxiety and expectations. If they are channelled positively, they can fuel purpose and drive transformation, but they can also pull people back, filling them with limiting thoughts. We have a situation in Edgard's case where a childhood incident heavily marked Edgard's identity and that of his brothers and paved a road of recognition and appreciation for William and Bruce, and one of self-deprecation and continuous micro-aggressions for Edgard. In spite of the warmth and supportive environment provided at home, Edgard felt like a shadow of his brothers, a black sheep. He found a purpose to become a better being and achieve something he would be proud of, creating a personal mission he pursued with grit and conviction. A fundamental prerequisite to succeed in a Deliberate Coaching Journey is the conviction to achieve results to improve your personal mission. This makes all the hurdles bearable and the journey exciting. Edgard had the key ingredients in him for a fulfilling future.

With the little nephews Jonny and Romy, we wanted to represent not only the additional attachment and expectation that Edgard would be committing to (for instance, by voicing over and making explicit his intention to achieve something big) but, most importantly, the simplicity of the narrative. Deliberate Coaching is a powerful methodology with transformational power at a large scale, yet at the core, the narrative must be simple, so much so that even children should be able to understand. The whys that every coachee would face, especially during moments of high pressure, should be talking to our inner child; the stories of heroes overcoming hurdles should feel like a kid's movie.

THE CASE FOR CHANGE: IGNITING THE INTERNAL FIRE

There are several ways in which coaching engagements can start. In ideal cases, the need comes from the individual eager for a change, and even more ideal if there is a conviction to work hard and go the extra mile to achieve it. In other cases (very common as well), the engagement is initiated by an external party vested in the individual success. Think of a direct manager or head of talent development taking a stance to support the career progression of top talented executives or, on the other spectrum, to manage underperforming individuals to support a step change. This latter approach requires the buy-in of the individual to be successful and, thus, is statistically less effective in driving individual change.

In our story, the case is initiated by Rita, Edgard's new manager, prompted by the relevancy of the project and the risk assessment of the cost of bringing a new manager to take over. It was understandably a difficult situation: Edgard, a high achiever and star hire for his credentials, suddenly burns his chances by putting in long hours and antagonising the team, all of which puts the most important project of the company (probably in history) at risk. The case merited some form of intervention, and Rita had the courage to attempt one.

In spite of the apparent transactional nature, the conditions were created and two bright professionals were connected to initiate a Deliberate Journey.

Notwithstanding that, the connection and transactions alone are not enough. The turning point was the conversation between Albert and Edgard at Edgard's place, while he was still on leave shortly after he was discharged from the hospital. Albert personified a great coaching professional and used that moment to build rapport, get to know Edgard better and learn and understand (by active listening) his motivations, desires and general mental models. He created a safe environment, and it didn't take much for Edgard to trust the coach in front of him. Both being high achievers and open to learning, they realised that the upside was large and the journey could be filled with tons of self-discovery. They contracted and agreed after building trust and understanding each other's motivations – the fundamental first milestone of Deliberate Coaching.

THE CALL: WHEN PREPARATION FINDS AN OPPORTUNITY

From the angle of the coach, a relevant development of the story occurs when Rita contacts Albert to take the "case" and support Edgard in turning the project around and himself. Albert represents the life of many coaches convinced of the transformational nature of their professions but have to deal with several Headwinds to build and sustain a scalable business. Stigma, lack of awareness and misleading assumptions to "go and fix the employee" are common manifestations. Albert summarises his stance and reserves the right to work with Edgard, provided his conversation shows that Edgard has the right attitude to engage.

In spite of the structural challenges, we wanted to portray the power of reputation and word-of-mouth, as Rita found outstanding recommendations for the work Albert was doing and his new practice called Deliberate Coaching. This is the first time the methodology finds its way into the narrative.

DEFINING THE HEART

From the Deliberate Methodology, the HEART is the goal – the reason to change. If achieved, the personal state will unleash a sense of satisfaction and completeness like nothing else for that individual. Defining it should take at least one full session among the Coaching instances and follow a thorough process of relevant questions, active listening and empathy that the coach should orchestrate. In our story, the goal was articulated as:

I want to be recognised in the next Mud Spring Festival as the Prodigal Pig that builds a centre of Joy and sportsmanship to the world…

And synthesised as:

A Prodigal Triumph

Following the methodology, successful goals should have five elements:

They need to be explicit, very focused and use only a few words. Thoughts should be exciting and positively framed (this was emphasised with Edgard's reaction and body language while speaking). They should be measurable, which, in our case, is defined by building a physical element. They should be challenging and represent a stretch for the individual, which in our story is portrayed by Project Blue, one of its kind and the single largest project of the company in decades. Finally, it should be time-framed, which is represented by the reference to the festival, which occurs at a specific time of the year.

NAVIGATING THE PULSES

The chapters following the definition of the goals, represented as Sessions 2 to 4 are the instances where project milestones are discussed and reflected upon. They all have a similar structure. After building rapport and creating cordial space for conversation, the first part consists of reflecting on the tasks agreed upon in the previous session. Were they done? How difficult were they? What were the learnings? And then proceeding to update the Deliberate Journal or system used. Usually, these are great sources of insights since they are real and fresh examples of the individual owning the journey.

The second part of these conversations examines the future and probes into the weeks ahead. The coach tries to establish the actions to come and anticipates the different options to address the situation, encouraging Edgard to choose an approach. Finally, there is an articulation of the agreed tasks registered in the journal.

They take place in different settings (office, virtual, walking, restaurant) to illustrate the methodology's flexibility as long as it works for both the coach and coachee and offers an inviting environment for fulfilling exchanges.

Through these instances, Edgard conceives a way to unleash Bary's creativity to obtain a wonderful design, secures the cooperation from Susan to empower a young talent in her team to close the negotiations, realigns the role of Willy to fit the broader project better and creates the conditions for Mary to shine and demonstrates her leadership potential.

This all reaches a positive conclusion with the opening event in the stadium and the commissioning of the PetFlix Documentary.

The Time to Be Deliberate Is Now

*"Whether you think you can, or you think
you can't – you're right."*
Henry Ford

Congratulations! You have made it to the end. Your curious mindset served you well and vindicated what you have known all this time: You are special and have immense potential, and the power to unleash it lies within your inner self. It only needs a catalyst, a Deliberate one.

Deliberate Coaching is a methodology capable of releasing the best in anyone in the pursuit of a meaningful life goal. It combines the proven benefits of the coaching practice with the individual and collective benefits of delivering results. It connects accountable coaching practitioners with professionals full of conviction and passion for self-development. It creates a virtuous cycle of positive transformation and contagious energy for the coachee, the coach and the communities they belong to. It propagates HEARTS and PULSES at scale.

Writing the book was a deliberate goal for us. Doubts of our capabilities to articulate thoughts into words, perceived challenges about available time to fit with our daily jobs and family lives, and other limiting factors were challenges we faced, but the dream for the possibilities and the passion we have for personal development certainly won the race – at least the first leg. The next one was won the moment you reached this chapter, in the knowledge we now share. The final race, however, will be won when we can break stigmas and make coaching, in association, Deliberate Coaching, well known everywhere.

So, we ask you to become an agent of change in your life in the first place. Embrace your inner Edgard-the-Pig and find your Albert to formally kick-start a Deliberate Coaching Journey. After that, become a beacon of possibilities and positivism and spread the learnings with your friends and colleagues.

You can find additional resources and services
in our practice at **deliberate-coaching.com**

The time is now.
The best version of yourself awaits.

Notes

About the Authors

JAVIER ROSALES is a dynamic executive coach and change catalyst, driven to unlock the full potential of leaders and their teams. With a customer-centric mindset and a proven track record of delivering sustainable results, Javier brings a wealth of cross-industry experience to his transformative work.

As a seasoned consultant with stints at McKinsey & Co, Procter & Gamble, and Amazon, Javier possesses a deep understanding of the mindset and strategies required to navigate complex, large-scale change. He blends this operational expertise with a passion for people development, using evidence-based coaching techniques to help clients cultivate the resilience, collaboration, and self-driven ownership needed to thrive amid uncertainty. Javier also holds an MBA from the University of Cambridge.

Whether guiding executives through major organizational shifts or facilitating breakthrough sessions for high-performing teams, Javier's approach is both practical and empathetic. He works closely with clients to uncover limiting beliefs, build essential skills, and fortify the adaptive capacity to deliver sustainable impact. His ability to translate data-driven insights into meaningful, people-centered solutions sets him apart.

Based in London, Javier's global experience further enhances his coaching prowess. Having lived, studied, and worked in over 10 countries, he brings a multicultural fluency and sensitivity to his engagements. He expertly navigates diverse contexts, empowering international teams to align around a shared vision and overcome cross-cultural barriers. Javier is also a proud father of two beautiful girls.

Underpinning Javier's professional accomplishments is a steadfast commitment to personal growth and balance. An avid tennis player and astronomy enthusiast, he models the value of cultivating a fulfilling life beyond the workplace. This ethos of holistic development permeates his work, as he helps leaders find the courage to take bold action while maintaining their wellbeing.

Whether partnering with established enterprises or high-potential startups, Javier's mission is to catalyze transformation and build future-fit organizations. If you're navigating a critical inflection point, he would be honored to support your journey.

JOSE ENRIQUE (Kike) GONZATTI is a dynamic Change Delivery Leader and Executive Coach, passionate about creating spaces where global organizations can find the intersection between their vision, identity, strategy, and execution that lead to continuous performance improvement and sustainable change. With a core belief that people are the perfect catalyst for positive impact and success, Kike has always felt attracted to teaching and coaching from school years (was teacher assistant at undergrad level and Venezuela's tennis coach for the team going to the 2003 Special Olympics in Dublin), and has been fortunate to find the space in his professional life to continue and expand that trajectory, making it over 3 decades of experience of insipiring personal change.

Kike holds a business degree with an especialisation in Marketing, an MBA from IE University and additional studies in Change Management and Leadership from Oxford University and Wharton School. Throughout his career, Kike has leveraged every opportunity to act as an Executive Leadership Coach and visiting lecturer on Leadership and Change Management, fueled by his passion for connecting with others and his curious mindset.

Kike's extensive experience as a managing consultant for top firms like Accenture, Deloitte, and NTTDATA has given him deep insights into supporting global banks in designing and implementing transformative operating models. From this, he has learned the importance of leading by example with authenticity, using coaching as a tool to cultivate growth in those around him while also pushing himself to continuously improve. Most importantly, Kike prioritizes self-compassion at every stage of the journey.

Born and raised in Venezuela, he now lives in London with his wife and two children. Outside of his professional pursuits, he enjoys exercising, building Legos, spending time with family, and connecting with people from all walks of life. Kike feels deeply grateful for the growth opportunities he has experienced, including life-threatening situations, which have only reinforced his calling to serve and drive positive change in society.

Whether partnering with global enterprises or purpose-driven organizations, Kike's mission is to inspire transformation and cultivate the conditions for sustainable high performance. If you're navigating a critical inflection point, he would be honored to support your journey.

Thank You

Thank you for reading our book.

We really appreciate all of your feedback, and we love hearing what you have to say.

We need your input to make the next version of this book and our future books even better.

Please leave us a helpful review on Amazon letting us know what you thought of the book.

Thank you so much!
Javier Rosales and Jose E. Gonzatti